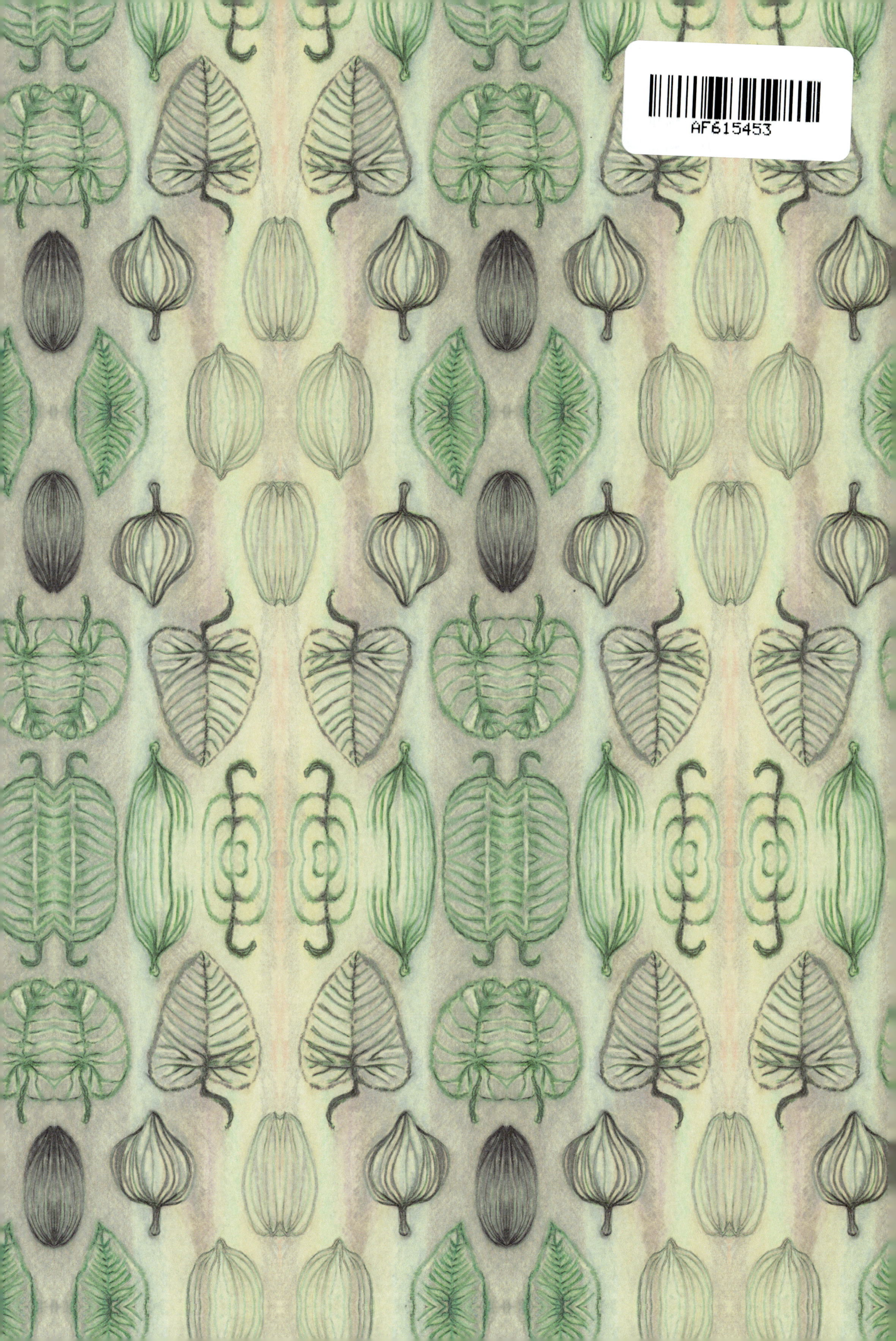

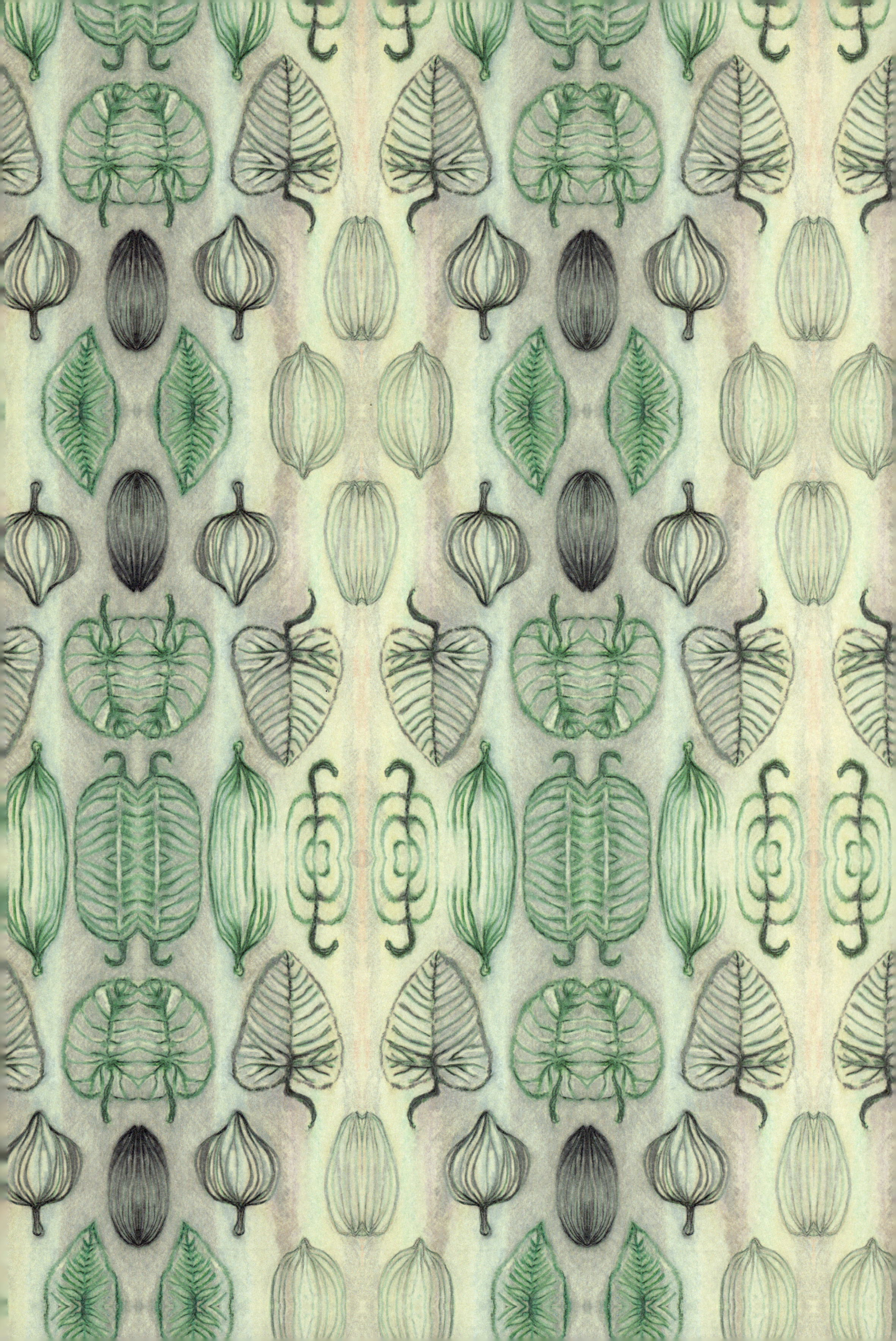

a different STATE of mind
Amy Simon

# a different STATE of mind
# Amy Simon

WITH TEXTS BY DANIEL BIRNBAUM
AND AMY BAKER SANDBACK

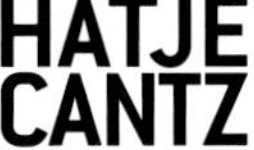

Society is indeed a contract. It is a partnership in all science; a partnership in all art; a partnership in every virtue, and in all perfection. As the ends of such a partnership cannot be obtained in many generations, it becomes a partnership not only between those who are living, but between those who are living, those who are dead, and those who are to be born.

Edmund Burke

Our world is so limited and small—our relativity is only experiential. We function within knowledge of our experiences of past and present, thereby creating our personal future.

Our experiences and therefore subsequent memories of them create and re-create our reality. And that reality becomes our world—and our world will never be isolated, it will always gather elements from a universal experience, therefore there will always be something in (my) images that can be identified with and then relate and built upon in "stories" from other's lives.

Amy Simon

# Contents

# Not At Home: Solitude, Melancholy, and Mirrors (for Amy Simon)

DANIEL BIRNBAUM

A closed door, the key still in the lock. The lurid bundle of keys marks the place where, perhaps, one could leave. We do get a glimpse of an outside, but can we be sure it exists? There are traces of social life, hints that outside of these walls there is a city, but in the end, only one person is at home. She is also only glimpsed at, but she is there. Is this really a *home* or, rather, a place of seclusion, even isolation? A cut-off realm for meditation or, rather, a place you are locked in? Is there a sense of claustrophobia?

Upon entering a particular apartment, from the 40 degree heat and the sunshine at 9:00 a.m. on a weekday morning, Amy Simon knew that more existed in this space for her, to her, about her, than just the architecture of the rooms. The light, the temperature, the odors all convinced her that she has had similar experiences. By photographing interiors only, and at times, exteriors from the inside looking out, the rooms became isolated from space and time. They became their own special world, cut off from the goings on of a greater universe. It was though a sense of utopia had been created, even though the visuals were as far from the ideals of a perfect world as they could be.

So is this really a home? In "The Uncanny" (1919), one of the most legendary of attempts to explore the richness of the word "home," Sigmund Freud utilizes the etymological dictionary:

*"The German word 'unheimlich' is obviously the opposite of 'heimlich' ['homely'], 'heimisch' ['native'] the opposite of what is familiar; and we are tempted to conclude that what is 'uncanny' is frightening precisely because it is not known and familiar.* Deutschlateinisches buch, 1898). An uncanny place: locus suspectus; at an uncanny time of night: *intempesta nocte.*
Greek: (Rost's and Schenkl's Lexikons). *Eeros* (i.e., strange, foreign).
English: (from the dictionaries of Lucas, Bellows, Flumlgel, and Muret-Sanders). Uncomfortable, uneasy, gloomy, dismal, uncanny, ghastly; (of a house) haunted; (of a man) a repulsive fellow.
French: (Sachs-Villatte). Inquiétant, sinistre, lugubre, mal à son aise.
Spanish: (Tollhausen, 1889). Sospechoso, de mal aguëro, lúgubre, siniestro.

The Italian and Portuguese languages seem to content themselves with words, which we should describe as circumlocutions. In Arabic and Hebrew, 'uncanny' means the same as 'daemonic,' 'gruesome.'

For compounds see above, Ic. Note especially the negative '*un-*': eerie, weird, arousing gruesome fear: 'Seeming quite *unheimlich* and ghostly to *him*.' 'The *unheimlich*, fearful hours of night.' 'I had already long since felt an *unheimlich*, *even* gruesome feeling.' 'Now I am beginning to have an *unheimlich* feeling.' ... 'Feels an *unheimlich* horror.' '*Unheimlich* and motionless like a stone image.' 'The *unheimlich* mist called hill-fog.' 'These pale youths are *unheimlich* and are brewing heaven knows what mischief.' '*Unheimlich is the name for everything that ought to have remained ... secret and hidden but has come to light*' (Schelling).—'To veil the divine, to surround it with a certain *Unheimlichkeit*.'—*Unheimlich* is not often used as opposite to meaning II (above)."[1]

What interests us most in this long extract is to find that among its different shades of meaning, the word *heimlich* exhibits one which is identical with its opposite, *unheimlich*. What is *heimlich*, thus, comes to be *unheimlich*. (Cf. the quotation from Gutzkow: 'We call it "*unheimlich*"; you call it "*heimlich*.") In general we are reminded that the word *heimlich* is not unambiguous, but belongs to two sets of ideas, which, without being contradictory, are yet very different: on the one hand it means what is familiar and agreeable, and on the other, what is concealed and kept out of sight. *Unheimlich* is customarily used, we are told, as the contrary only of the first signification of *heimlich*, and not of the second. Sanders tells us nothing concerning a possible genetic connection between these two meanings of *heimlich*. On the other hand, we notice that Schelling says something that throws quite a new light on the concept of the *Unheimlich*, for which we were certainly not prepared. According to him, everything is *unheimlich* that ought to have remained secret and hidden but has come to light.

Some of the doubts that have thus arisen are removed if we consult Grimm's dictionary (1877, 4. Part 2, pp. 873ff.). We read:

"*Heimlich;* adj. and adv. *vernaculus, occultus;* MHG, heimelich, heimlich.

(p. 874.) In a slightly different sense: 'I feel *heimlich*, well, free from fear.'...

[3] (b) *Heimlich* is also used of a place free from ghostly influences ... familiar, friendly, intimate.

(p. 875: ß) Familiar, amicable, unreserved."

From the idea of 'homelike,' 'belonging to the house,' the further idea is developed of

"*something withdrawn from the eyes of strangers, something concealed, secret; and this idea is expanded in many ways ...*

(p. 876.) 'On the left bank of the lake there lies a meadow *heimlich* in the wood.' (Schiller, *Wilhelm Tell,* 1.4.) ... Poetic license, rarely so used in modern speech ... *Heimlich* is used in conjunction with a verb expressing the act of concealing: 'In the secret of his tabernacle he shall hide me *heimlich.*' (Ps. xxvii. 5.) ... *Heimlich* parts of the human body, *pudenda* ... 'the men that died not were smitten on their *heimlich* parts.' (1 Samuel v. 12.) ...

(p. 878.) 6. *Heimlich,* as used of knowledge—mystic, allegorical: a *heimlich* meaning, *mysticus, divinus, occultus, figuratus.*

(p. 878.) *Heimlich* in a different sense, as withdrawn from knowledge, unconscious ... *Heimlich* also has the meaning of that which is obscure, inaccessible to knowledge ... 'Do you not see? They do not trust us; they fear the *heimlich* face of the Duke of Friedland.' (Schiller, *Wallensteins Lager,* Scene 2.)

9. *The notion of something hidden and dangerous, which is expressed in the last paragraph, is still further developed, so that 'heimlich' comes to have the meaning usually ascribed to 'unheimlich.'* Thus: 'At times I feel like a man who walks in the night and believes in ghosts; every corner is heimlich and full of terrors for him.' (Klinger, *Theater,* 3. 298.)

Freud concludes: "Thus, *heimlich* is a word the meaning of which develops in the direction of ambivalence, until it finally coincides with its opposite, *unheimlich. Unheimlich* is in some way or other a sub-species of *heimlich.*" The reality was that the occupant of the apartment was an immigrant, as Simon is, and her family had been in the past. But in that moment, the occupant was the immigrant to this particular city, to this apartment, which was evident by those conditions that can be felt in the atmosphere and, therefore, depicted in the things that could been seen and were obvious in the décor. How to sum up the experiences of an individual, a generation, a people is difficult in words, but there exist certain commonalities in emotion that can be sensed on a non-verbal level and visualized.

May we conclude: Being home means being in a foreign place?

*

A closed door, the key still in the lock. The lurid bundle of keys marks the place where, perhaps, one could leave. We do get a glimpse of an outside, but can we be sure it exists? There are traces of social life, hints that outside of these walls there is a city, but in the end only one person is at home. She is also only glimpsed at, but she is there. Is this really a *home* or, rather, a place of seclusion, even isolation? A cut-off realm for meditation or, rather, a place you are locked in? Is there a sense of claustrophobia?

No, the isolation is of another kind. The philosophers of the Renaissance pointed out a close connection between creativity and melancholy: The soul of the artist is torn between the darkness of depression and the light of creativity. The night of the soul, from which the spark of genius springs, is a solitary darkness. The relation of melancholy to isolation and solitude is already suggested in ancient sources, but becomes a central topic in Renaissance treatises: The artist enters into himself, into an inner darkness, and there, finds the source of creativity. Robert Burton, in his comprehensive study, discusses the pathological desire of the melancholic for isolation, his misanthropic "no" to the world. Is melancholy the result of solitude? Or is the desire for isolation a result of the melancholy? Burton never answers the question unequivocally, but the kinship of the two phenomena is repeatedly stressed.

In Michel de Montaigne *Essays* from 1580, the relationship between solitude, melancholy, and creativity is dealt with in a way more thorough than we find elsewhere. Here, this relationship is described as the most basic precondition of writing: "It was a melancholic mood—that is, a mood that is the precise opposite of my natural disposition—elicited by the bleak solitude that I threw myself into a few years ago that instilled in me this crazy idea of writing. And then, when I discovered that I was completely empty and destitute of other subject matters, I took myself as subject and object of study."[2] Montaigne does not regard melancholy as his natural temperament, but rather, as a state into which he conveyed himself by radical isolation. His psychic disposition is, in point of fact, mixed, and thus—according to authorities of the time—ideal: "My temperament is between the jovial and the melancholic, moderately sanguine and warm."[3]

Melancholy arose from intentional isolation, from the decision to turn one's back on the world in order to devote the remainder of life to the cultivation of one's own soul. This introverted movement is a first precondition for writing. It is by means of solitude that Montaigne becomes melancholic. And from the melancholy of the soul, the desire to write is born:

> When I recently retired to my home, determined, to the fullest extent possible, not to bother about anything other than spending the short life I have left to rest and seclusion, I believed that I could do my soul no greater service than to let it take care of itself in complete inactivity and let it make itself comfortable on its own. I assumed it would be easier for it now, because it has matured with time and has received a richer content. But on the contrary, I now find
>
> —*an idle life always produces varied inclinations* (Lucanus)—
>
> that the soul is behaving like a runaway horse and is a hundred times more concerned about itself than it previously had been about others. It gives birth to so many chimeras and fantastic monsters, one after another, that I, in order to ponder over their silliness and quirkiness in peace and quiet, have begun to write them down, with the hope that over time, I can get the soul to begin to be ashamed of itself.[4]

Melancholic madness arises from isolation: The imagination gallops away and creates fantastic monsters. The ego, or "I," is threatened with utter lunacy, but the "I" manages to stem the movement of the bolting horse by corralling the fantasies in writing. The ability of the written sign to fix the rushing images permits the "I" to find a new stability; the soul gets the opportunity to reflect on its creations. Writing means a rescue from the chaotic night of melancholy. This is Montaigne's circle: The soul turns away from the world and moves into itself. In the inner night, melancholy and madness threaten-but by means of writing, the soul can return to the world.

In *Montaigne en mouvement,* Jean Starobinski sees this circle as the most general motion of the essays: from a deep skepticism toward outer reality, there follows an emphasis on the inner life of the "I," an inner searching that, by means of the investigation itself, is able to return to the external reality that was initially negated.[5] This is the general pattern of the essays, but it is only the endless variations that give them their luster. The same melancholic trope recurs again and again, but with Montaigne's *Essays,* writes Starobinski, it is like a musical composition: "All the variations in a *chaconne* can be inferred from the first notes of the base, nonetheless, the piece is not finished until the entire development is complete."[6] Montaigne's music streams out from melancholy's night, but it is, nonetheless, not a death fugue; it is rather a composition about life rediscovered. It is about overcoming darkness and melancholy. Literature serves as the way back out into the light. What does the actual turning point look like? What is it about melancholy that makes this reversal possible?

Previous writers have discussed even this very critical point, and Montaigne is hardly the first to locate the inversion in the dark depths of the soul. "And the night was dark and lit up the night," we read in John of the Cross.[7] The idea that darkness, by being concentrated maximally, can produce a different kind of light is also found in alchemy, in which the pitch-black *nigredo phase* is a necessary phase in the production of the shimmering, brilliant gold. So the notion of inversion itself is not new, but Montaigne is the first to allow the overcoming of night and melancholy to coincide with the actual act of writing: by writing, the soul is saved from its darkness and solitude. Perhaps he could be called the first writer in the modern sense.[8] With Montaigne, writing becomes the solitary soul's deeply personal concern; the literary text arises from a personal crisis, but at the same time, writing is a rescuing from darkness.

Here, the Renaissance's *melancholia generosa* becomes a name for the positive turning point where the isolation is broken—where the silence of internal contemplation is transformed into writing. "I'm not actually melancholic, but dreamy," writes Montaigne, but adds: "There is nothing which I, from the very beginning, have devoted myself to more than fantasy images of death."[9] Melancholy occurs when the "I" isolates itself and gives itself over completely to its fantasies of death. The inner eclipse of the soul is imminent: The light of reason gives way to the night of madness. But solitude need not result in madness; it can also be cultivated, and can make possible contemplative depths. Montaigne stresses the necessity of solitude for all intellectual activity, not only an external solitude, but the soul's radical isolation: "This is why it is not enough to keep one's distance from the crowd, it is not enough to change location; we must get away from the mass that exists within ourselves. We have to withdraw and reclaim ourselves."[10]

By means of this phenomenological reduction, the "I" acquires access to an inner space, a separate place for deep philosophical meditation:

> We need to secure an inner space for ourselves that is ours alone, totally free, where we establish our real freedom, our most important refuge and solitude. It is here where our normal conversations between us and ourselves should take place, so personal that no external relations and connections may be present; here, we will be able to talk and laugh as if we had no wife, children, or possessions, no attendants or servants, so that there will not be anything new for us when the time comes when we lose them. We have a soul that can turn to itself, it can keep itself company, it can attack and defend, receive and give away; let us not fear, then, that we in this solitude will stagnate from boring idleness: If you are in a solitary place, be a mass for yourself![11]

Seclusion is necessary for the philosophical person. But it brings with it melancholy's ambivalence of mind. Montaigne is surely familiar with the classical view of the dual nature of melancholy: "Plato says that melancholiacs are the most educable and prominent—but at the same time, no others have such a clear disposition to madness. Countless spirits have been demolished under their own power and adroitness."[12] Solitude is dangerous, but indispensable. Montaigne himself withdraws back to his secluded tower, where he can cultivate his melancholy in peace and quiet. It never degenerates into madness, but rather, is resisted and ennobled into writing.

*

A closed door, the key still in the lock. The lurid bundle of keys marks the place where, perhaps, one could leave. We do get a glimpse of an outside, but can we be sure it exists? There are traces of social life, hints that outside of these walls there is a city, but in the end only one person is at home. She is also only glimpsed at, but she is there. Is this really a *home* or, rather, a place of seclusion, even isolation? A cut-off realm for meditation or, rather, a place you are locked in? Is there a sense of claustrophobia?

About the monad, the simple substance in Leibniz's philosophy, Gilles Deleuze writes: "The monad is a cell. It resembles a sacristy more than an atom: a room with neither doors nor windows, where all activity takes place on the inside."[13] It's an infinitely simple and, at the same time, endlessly complex structure. A space closed from the world, yet containing everything: a perpetual mirror of the universe.

Our world is so limited and small says Simon, our relativity is only experiential. We function within knowledge of our experiences of past and present, thereby creating our personal future. Our experiences and therefore, subsequent memories of them create and re-create our reality. And that reality becomes our world-and our world will never be isolated, it will always gather elements from a universal experience. Therefore, there will always be something in images that can be identified with and then related to and built upon in "stories" from other's lives.

"Crystalline perfection lets no outside subsist: there is no outside of the mirror or the film set, but only an obverse where the characters who disappear or die go," states Deleuze when discussing the function of mirrors in the fabrication of "crystal images," those rare cinematic instants in which the very operation of time becomes visible."[14] Orson Welles offers some of the most powerful and perplexing examples. "Forms of multiplicity and incongruity abound in this film," asserts Jorge Luis Borges in a review of *Citizen Cane.*[15] He quotes Chesterton, saying that nothing is as frightening as a labyrinth without a center. "This film," he maintains, "is precisely this labyrinth." Kane himself, who famously passes between two opposing mirrors, is but a "simulacrum, a chaos of appearances." The following year, in 1942, he publishes "Death and the Compass," his own Kircherian fantasy about a detective who enters a house that seem infinite and expanding: "He ascended the dusty stairs to circular antechambers; he was multiplied infinitely in opposing mirrors."[16] Has he entered a maze of mirrors, perhaps a reconstruction of Kircher's "polydyptic theater"? '*The house is not this large,* he thought. *Other things are making it seem larger: the dim light, the symmetry, the mirrors, so many years, my unfamiliarity, the loneliness.*[17]

Sometimes the inside is larger than that outside and the isolated place turns out to be infinitely hospitable. The occupant of the apartment is an immigrant, just as the artist is in the present and her family has been in the past. Although seemingly cut off and isolated, the life of an individual always gather elements from a universal experience. No matter how unique, your story always relates to stories of others. Says Simon, "These works depict all that has past and the creation of all that can be; they hold the weight of the bearer and a multitude of possibilities." She is alone. She is not alone. Like all of us: She is at home, she is not at home.

---

1) Sigmund Freud, "The Uncanny," *The Standard Edition of the Complete Psychological Works of Sigmund Freud*, vol. xvii, ed. J. Strachey (London, 1919), pp. 219–52.
2) Michael de Montaigne, *Les Essais* (Paris, 2007), p. 78.
3) Ibid., p. 421.
4) Ibid., p. 46.
5) Jean Starobinski, *Montaigne en mouvement* (Paris, 1982).
6) Ibid., p. 9.
7) Saint John of the Cross, cited in Roland Barthes, *Fragments d'un discours amoureux* (Paris, 1977), p. 165.
8) For a discussion of Montaigne's originality and the relation between his *Essays* and Augustine's *Confessions*, see M. A. Screech, *Montaigne and Melancholy* (London, 1983).
9) *Montaigne*, (see note 2), p. 110.
10) Ibid. I, p. 295.
11) Ibid. I, pp. 297f.
12) Ibid. II, p. 214.
13) Gilles Deleuze, *Cinema 2: The Time-Image,* trans. Hugh Tomlinson and Roberta Galeta (London, 1989), p. 83.
14) Ibid.
15) Jorge Luis Borges, *Selected Non-Fictions*, ed. Eliot Weinberger (London, 1999), p. 259.
16) Jorge Luis Borges, *Labyrinths* (London, 1970), p. 114.
17) Ibid.

# Making Sense of It All

AMY BAKER SANDBACK

Some say that the devil is in the details. In the work of Amy Simon, the graphic fragments extracted from her photographs are bedevilments that pose a variety of possible meanings, although she provides full disclosure, and uses sharp focus in her telling references. That is what photography does: It "takes" a piece of reality, but only a segment, and it is the viewer who is required to connect broader meaning with imagery by following the artist's visual suggestions and implications to decode the meaning and reach an understanding. For all the factual information given to us, we must nonetheless rely on our own experience and intellect if we are to uncover agendas. Should there be any, for it is uncertain whether there are covert intentions on the part of the artist.

Simon practices this art of extraction from a brimming world of possibilities, and uses her camera to present transformations from the brew. In this art, the artist's interest is in bringing attention to small areas of reality frozen in time and stilled by the lens of her camera. The pictures are created in the moment that they are "taken" out, removed from the ongoing rush of events. We must decide if these images serve merely as isolated mementos, or if they represent larger truths outside their immediate frame of reference. The artist says that a mix of experience and memory direct her artwork: "It's all a matter of awareness, and how much you absorb as you go through life, and the constant 'job' of trying to make sense of it all." The imagery in these photographs and drawings may, therefore, appear objective, but all have been selected by the photographer in a highly subjective process. Her photographs are a cropped sampling. They stand fully on their own, even when removed from their usual context.

Simon's established working process is to take hundreds of pictures, later paring down the multitude to a few that hold her interest. The selection is then printed as 120 x 80 cm C-prints, a size directly related to the artist's own body. These dimensions also allow the viewer to experience the images at a roughly one-to-one scale. This formal presentation is only one aspect of the artist's concern. Also printed are informal working proofs over which a white paper frame is moved to locate areas from which the artist then generates drawings based on these fragments. Drawn freehand with colored pencils, the drawings, unlike the C-prints, are quite small, 10 x 5 cm. But, these dimensions also have a personal connection, being the size of the pocket sketchbook that Simon often carries on her travels. The technique in the drawings is very direct, and the notations are more akin to the emotional tone of personal snapshots than to the exactitude of pristine professional photographs. These are private markings by the artist that we are privileged to view only in part, as though viewed through a keyhole. Seeing behind the closed door of her thinking may lead to a room, an object, or another vantage point of reality, but to see into this world or view beyond one of her windows, we must follow her directions. In this work, one has the sensation of eavesdropping.

This sense of being an onlooker or outsider is particularly strong in the series of photographs and drawings titled *a different STATE of mind* that Simon exhibited at the Venice Biennale in 2009. The photographs were taken in Tel Aviv, but there is scant hint of the flavor of that city, and although the imagery is domestic (views of an apartment), there is no immediacy to suggest the imprint of a home or family. In some images, we see the figure of a young girl passing in and out of the frame without explanation, or any apparent purpose, or connection to the environment. A hall opens onto a room with a window with a sheer white curtain in bright light; there is a black-and-white patterned floor, a lamp by a sofa, the lacy edge of a curtain at the side of a window, and on another window, long and thin, and partly obscured by two sheets of paper with the green of trees seen at the lower portion where there is a grille. There is also a window without a curtain, or grille, or view that looks across to yet another empty window. It is a generic place that one could find in many locales in the world. We are only granted partial access and must be content to see some, but not all, of the building's space inside and out. Among the images in the *Epilogue* to the series, not included in the Venice exhibition, are two photographic still lifes, one composed of items on a shelf, bottles, an empty vase, a plant; and the other, of differing-sized glass—never was the term "still life" more appropriate.

In fact, the apartment houses an immigrant, a person between old and new locations, one who is not yet grounded in her current residence. There is no real warmth here, rather simply habitation, and only the suggestion of occupation. The girl who passes by does not touch anything. All is silent. To enter this space we go through a white painted metal door from which a set of keys, each one color encoded, is hanging from the lock. The image of the door and keys became the source for a drawing, originally very small, which was then enlarged to cover an entire wall at the Venice exhibition. Measuring 7 x 6 m, this image is far beyond the human scale discussed above, and is in contradiction to the comfortable size of the photographs or the intimacy of the drawings. The mural is the result of a triple play: First, the set of keys was photographed, then a detail from the photograph selected and used as the basis for a small colored pencil drawing, and finally, the drawing was scanned and printed in a very large format. The small detail that is the subject matter becomes monumental. In order to read the enlargement, the viewer has to back away, thereby obscuring the complexity of the full

»Alle Kunst ist der Freude gewidmet.«

*“All art is dedicated to joy.”*

*Friedrich Schiller*

composition. Seen close up, the image reads as an abstract rather than as a drawing of keys in a lock.

These artworks move from the general to the particular. Reducing a situation or image to its constituent parts is often crucial in order to reach a better understanding of its meaning. One can gain insight by paying attention to the details as well as to the general context. How else can we seek to anchor ourselves in the confusion of a crowded reality? Separating something from its mooring can enhance this connection. To take away, to withdraw, is an abstraction which is defined historically as "a small quantity containing the virtue or power of the great" as well as "the act or process of separating in thought, of considering a thing independently of its associations." It is a distillation, in this case, a partial piece of information examined in service of a better understanding of the whole.

The details of life presented in these artworks are important textures of thought that address questions of place and identity, but the facts of the matter are just the beginning. While the artist generously presents her discoveries and enlarges some of them to ease our viewing, at other times, she extracts a detail and makes a drawing based on it, to ensure that we do not overlook what is important. It is up to us to take her suggestions and decode them. "Withdrawal" can mean a retirement or displacement, but in this instance, the forms of the withdrawal become the forms of an engagement that enable the artist to shape the artwork. Whether using a camera or colored pencils, diverting attention from the general to the particular, Simon uncovers entry points. As the artist has written, "Every time we view a photo, a chord is struck within each of us, resonating in anticipation of accompaniment of our own personal story or interpretation." Meaning and perception are inextricably connected. The artist seems to insist on personal involvement, ours as well as hers, to see the whole. We all participate according to our own histories.

# *a different STATE of mind*, No. 1–25

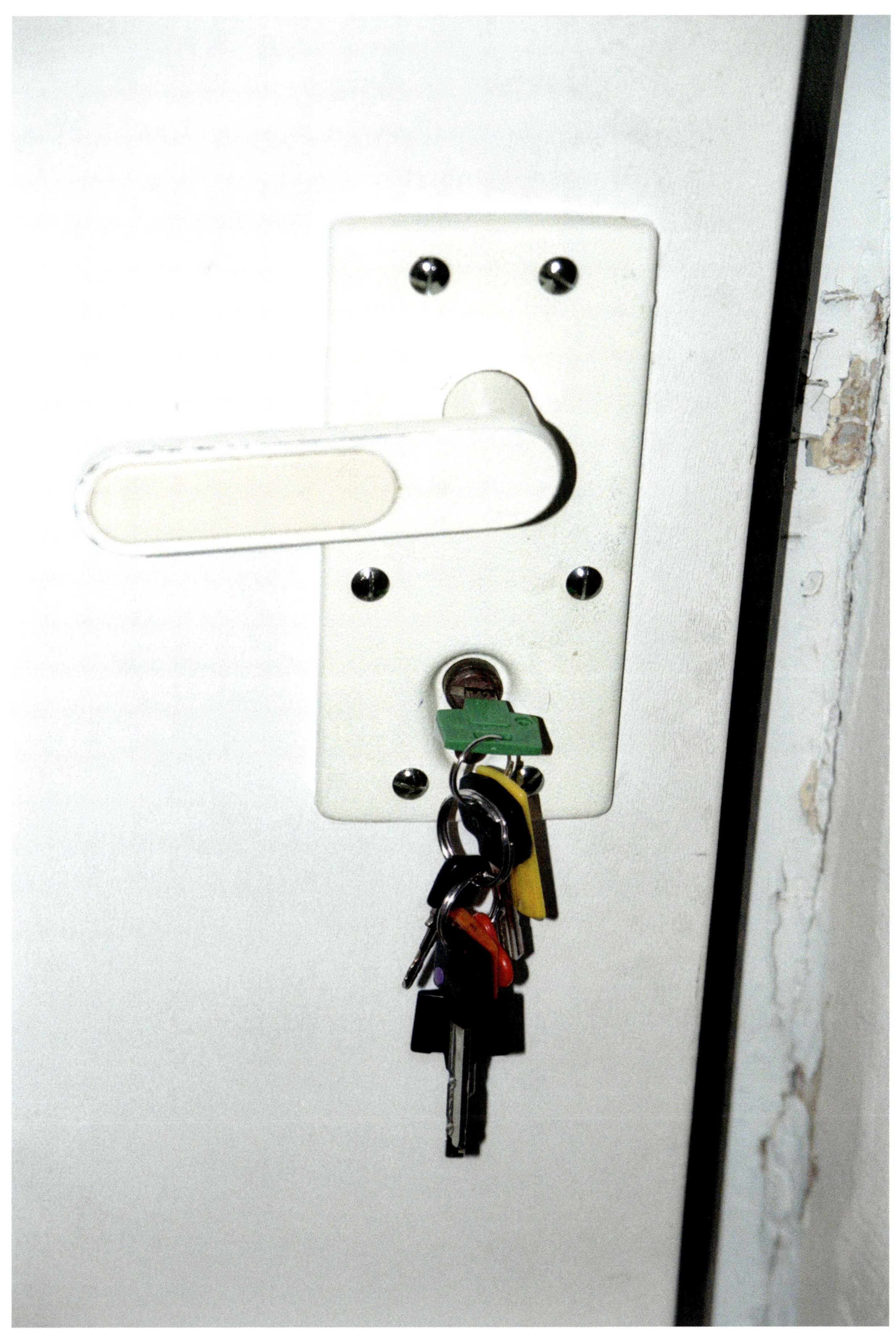

No. 2

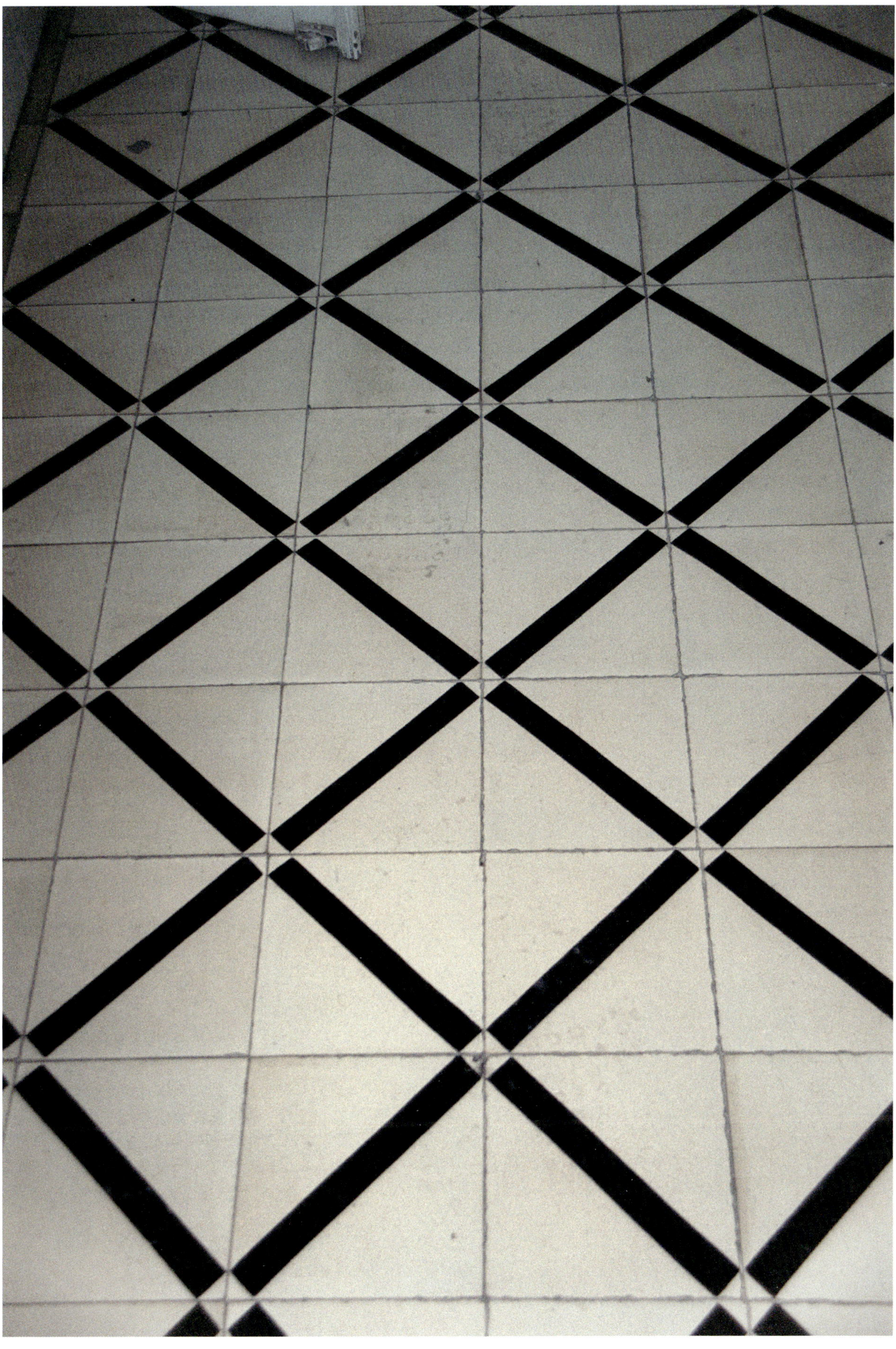

No. 13

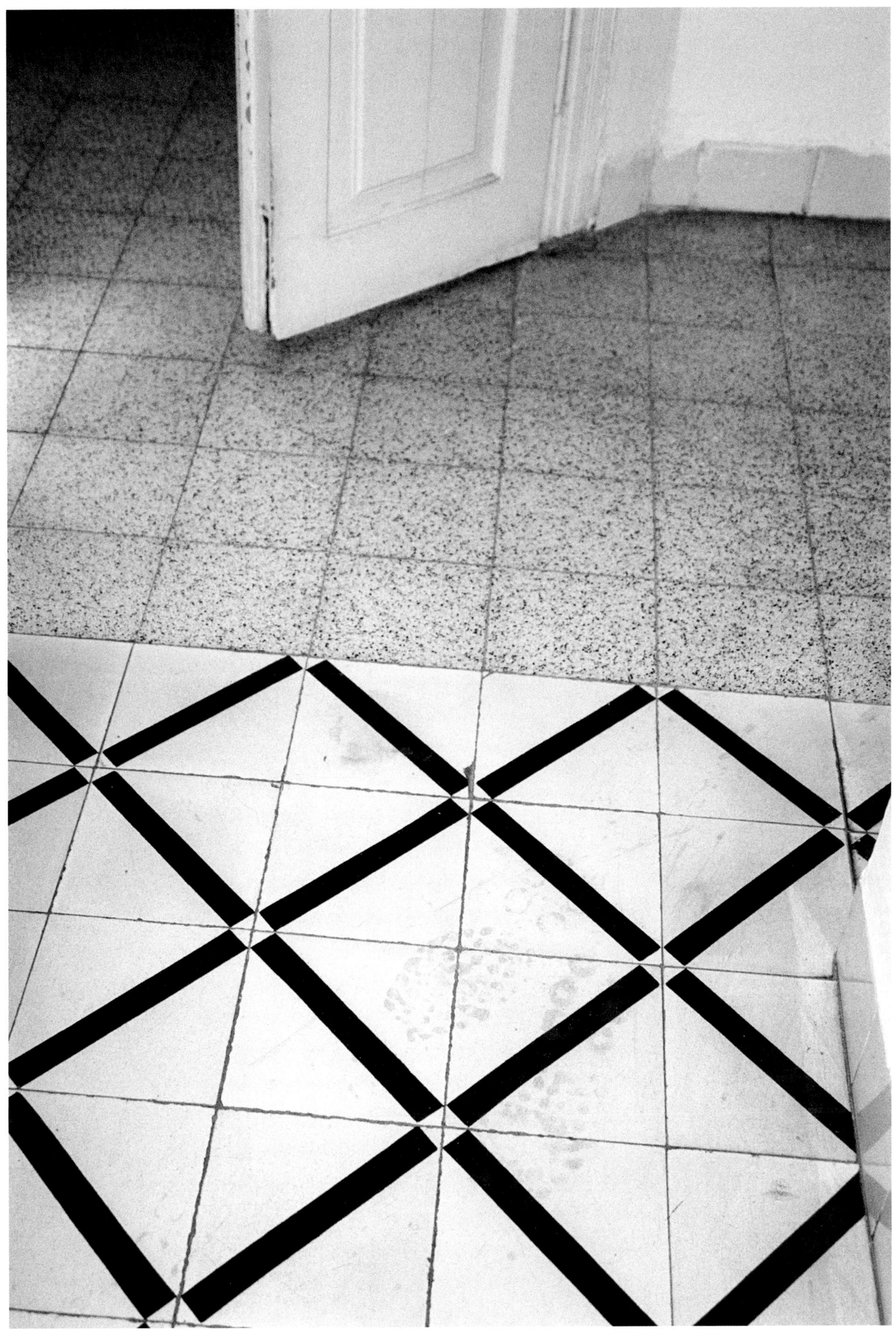

No. 24

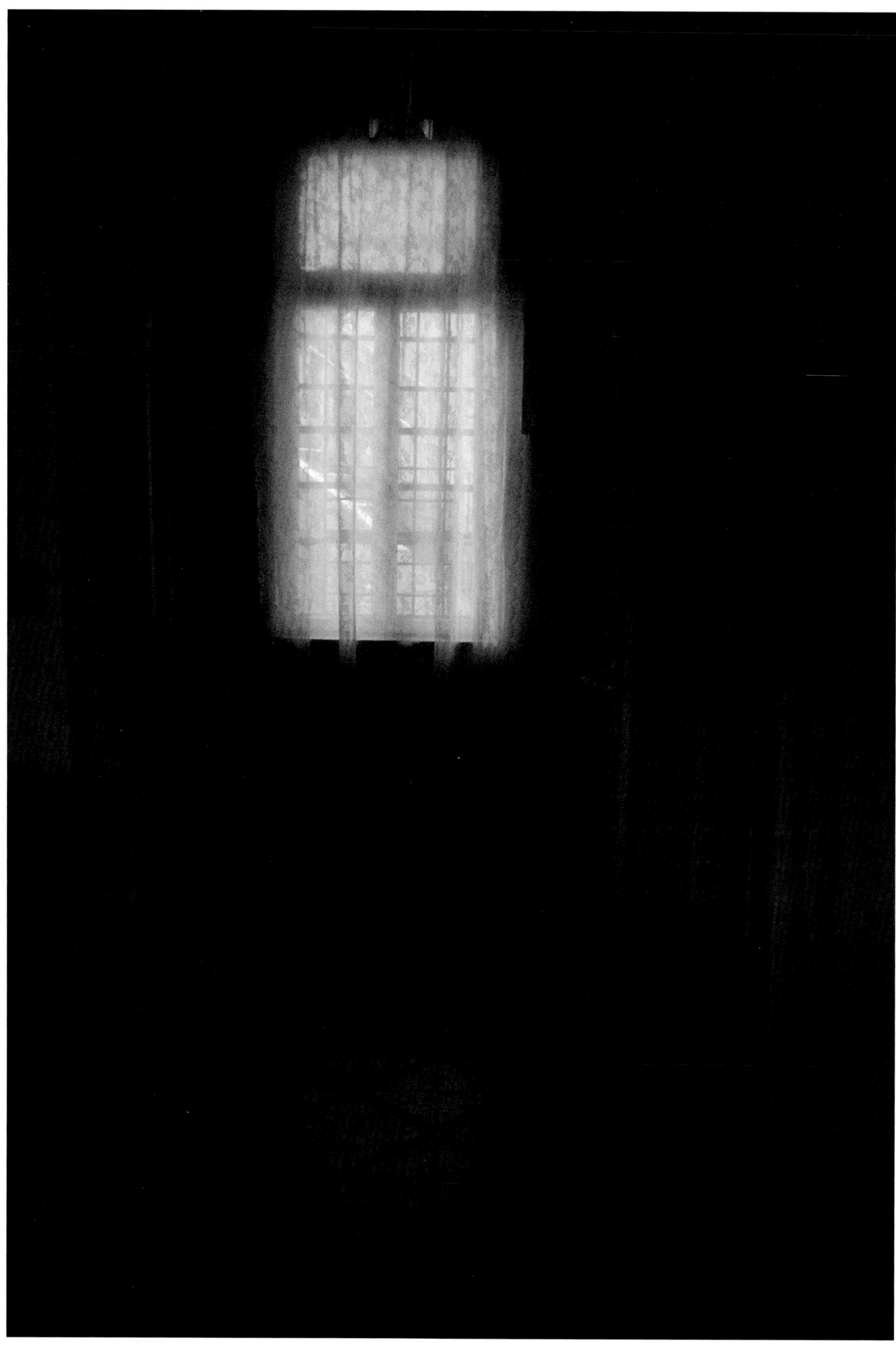



No. 10

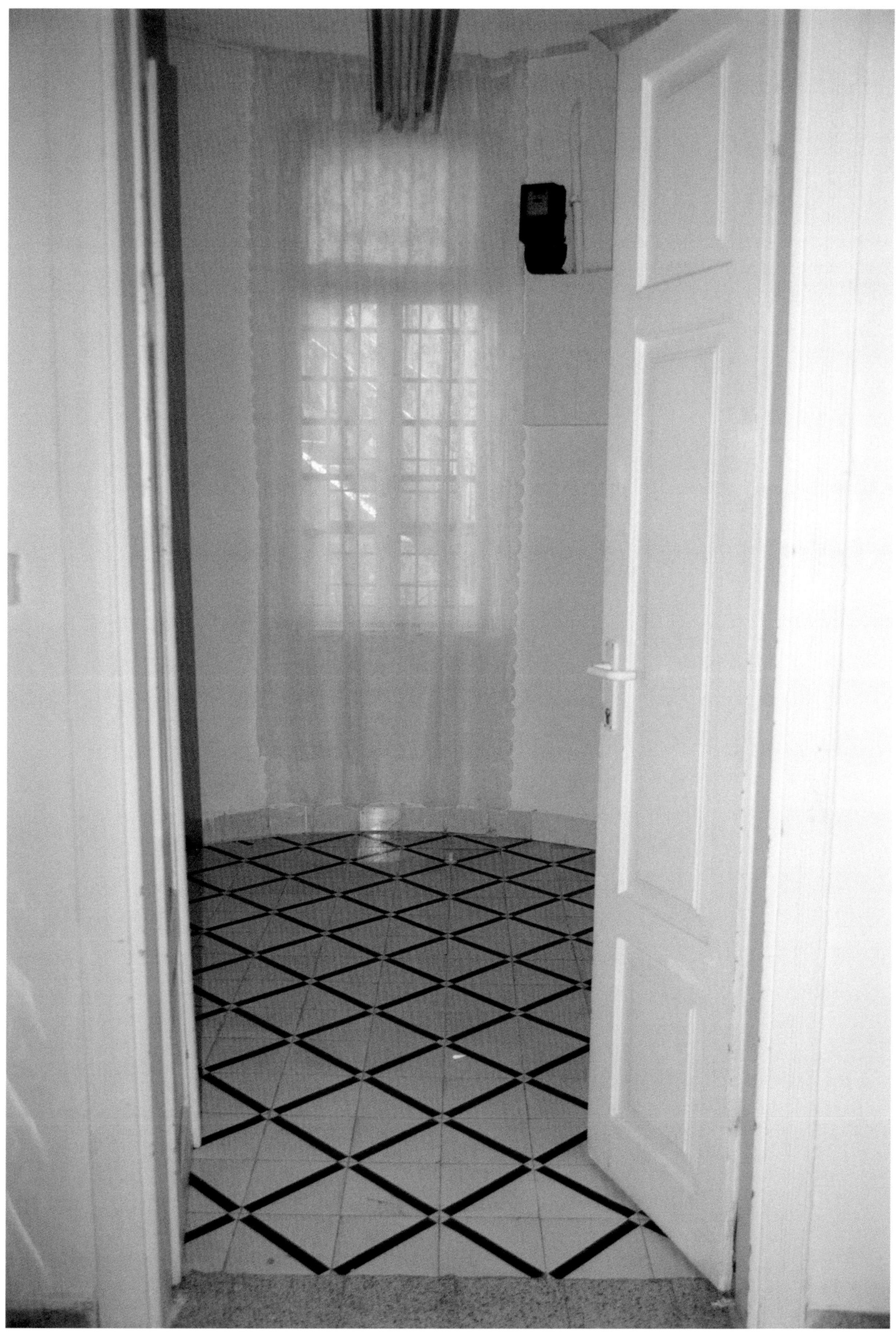

No. 11

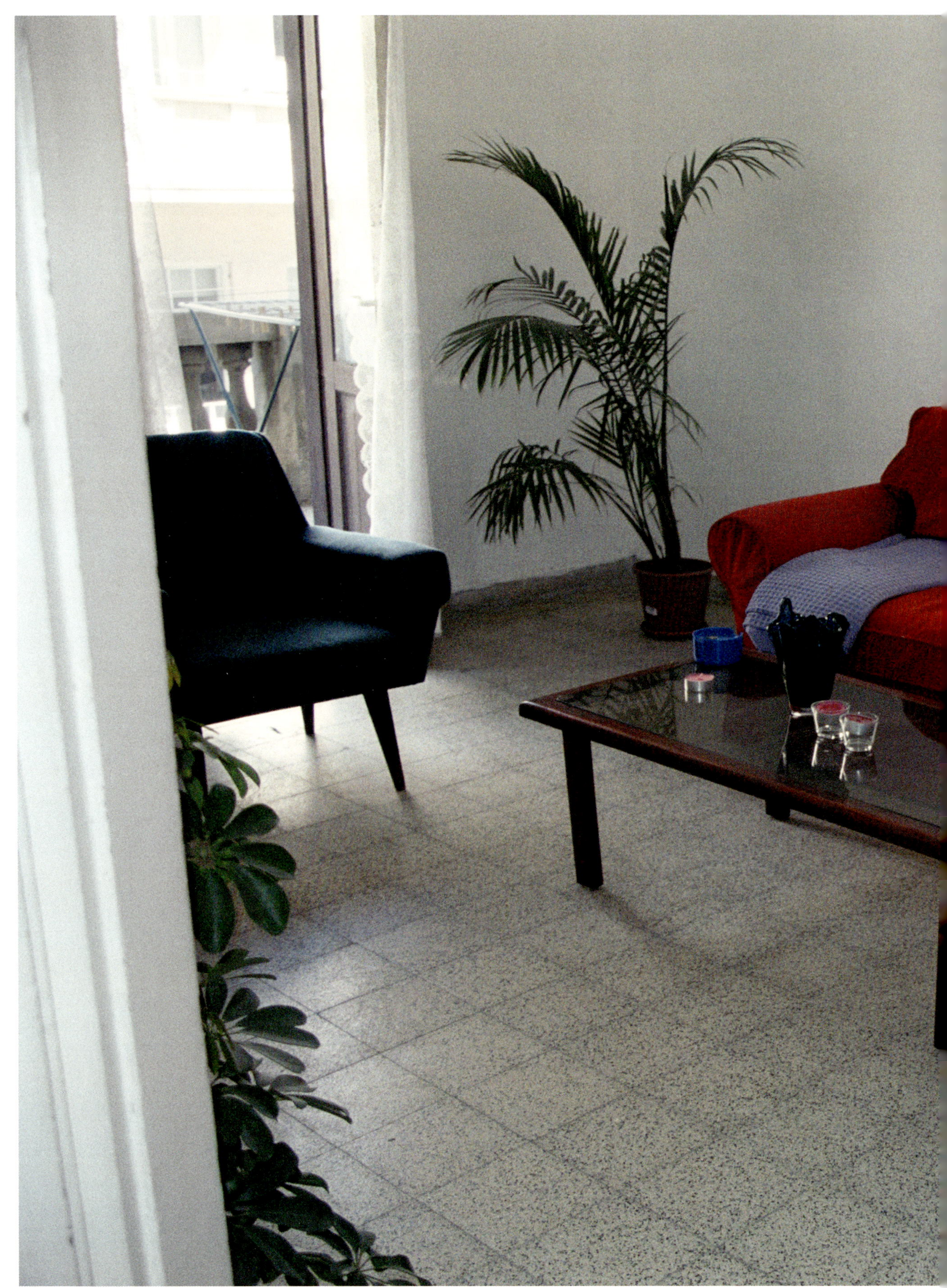

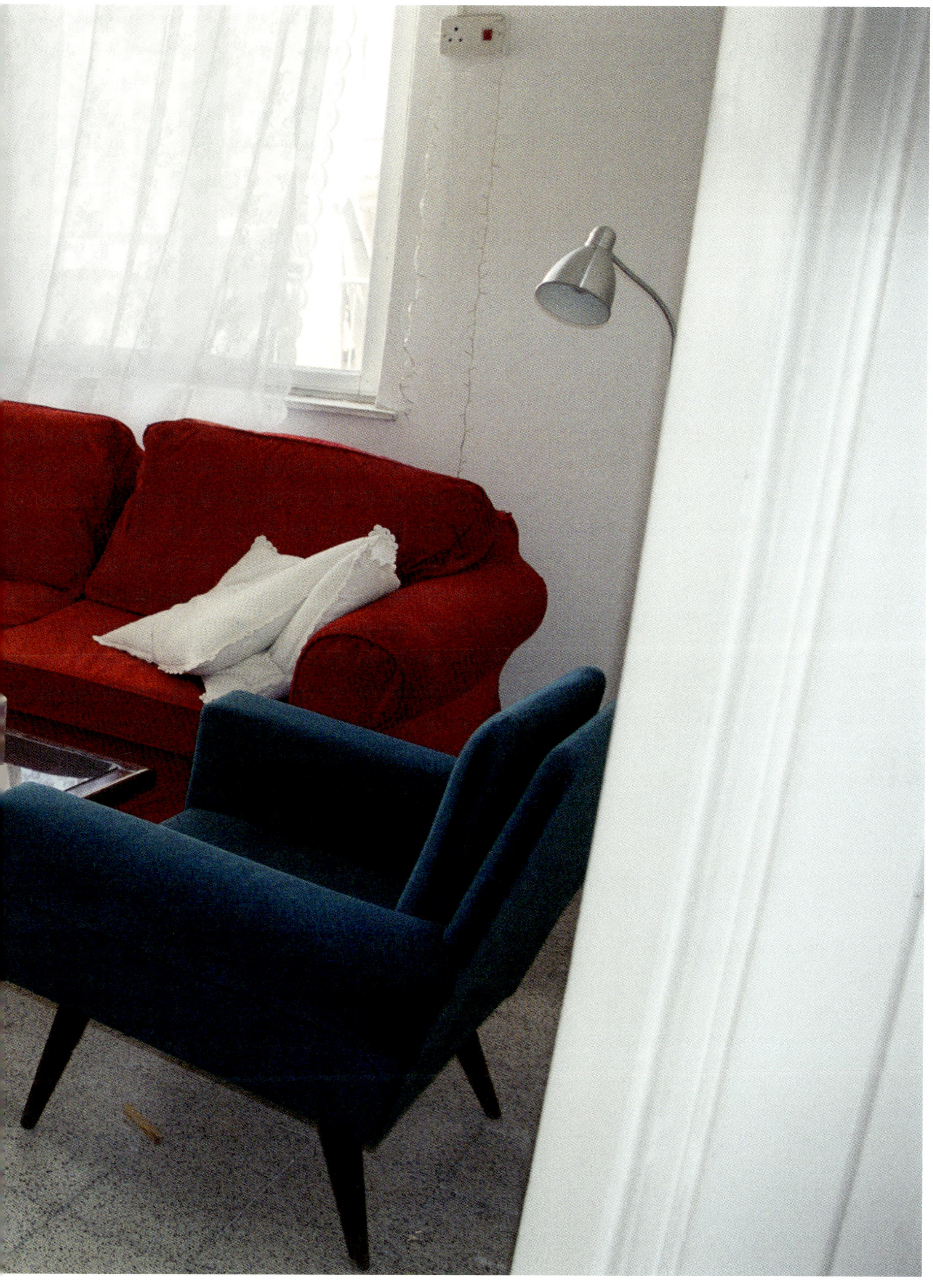

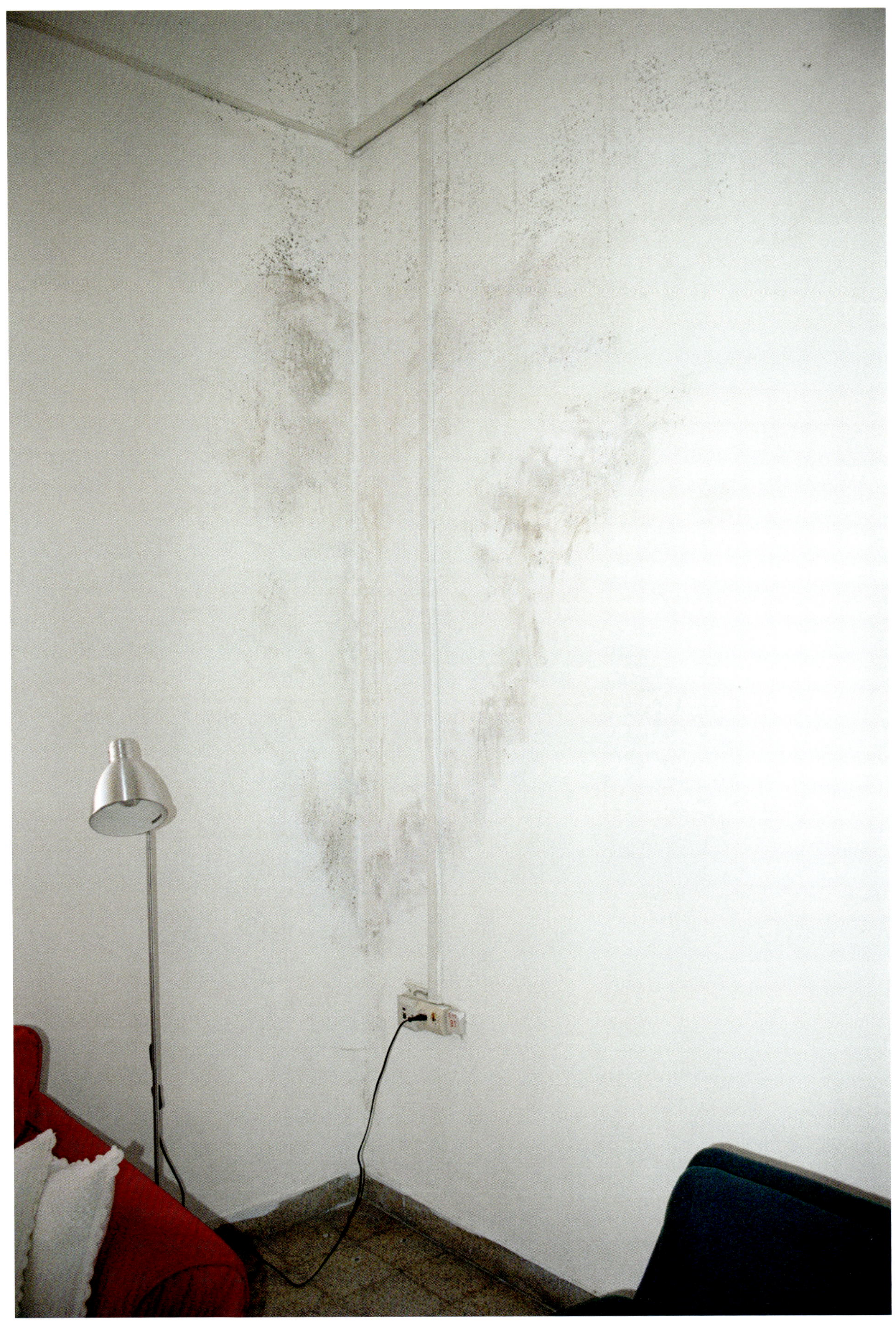



No. 8

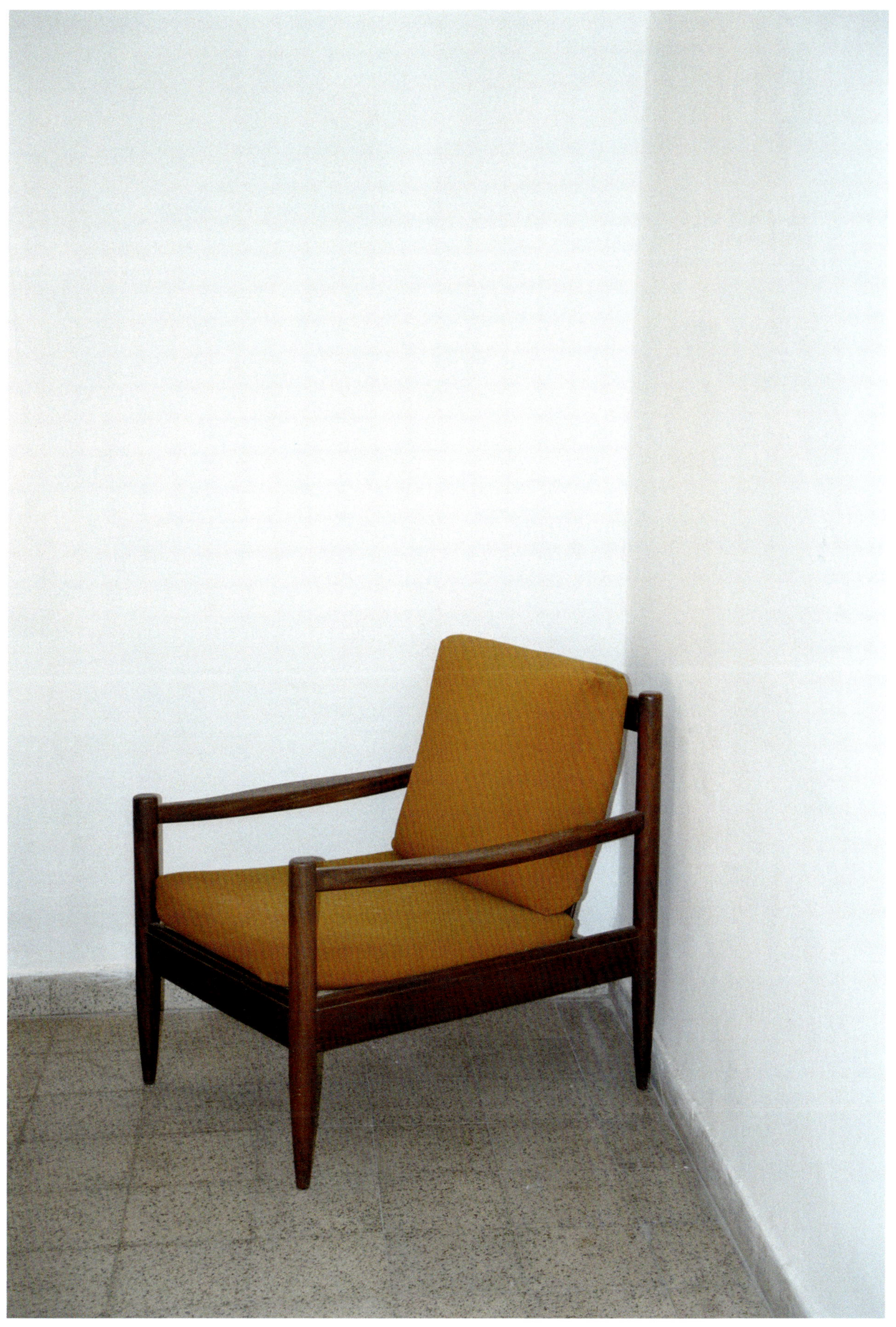

No. 4

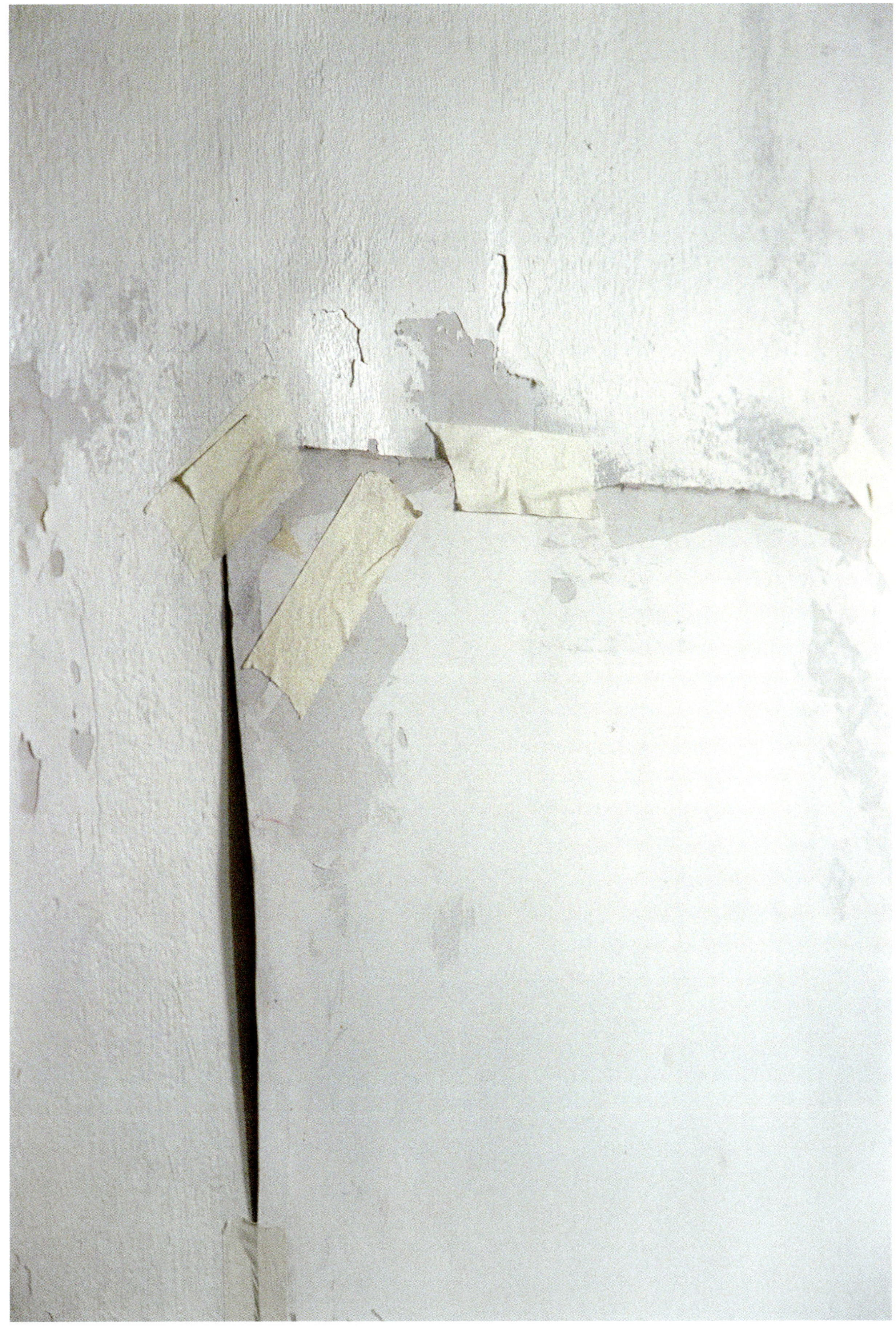

No. 20

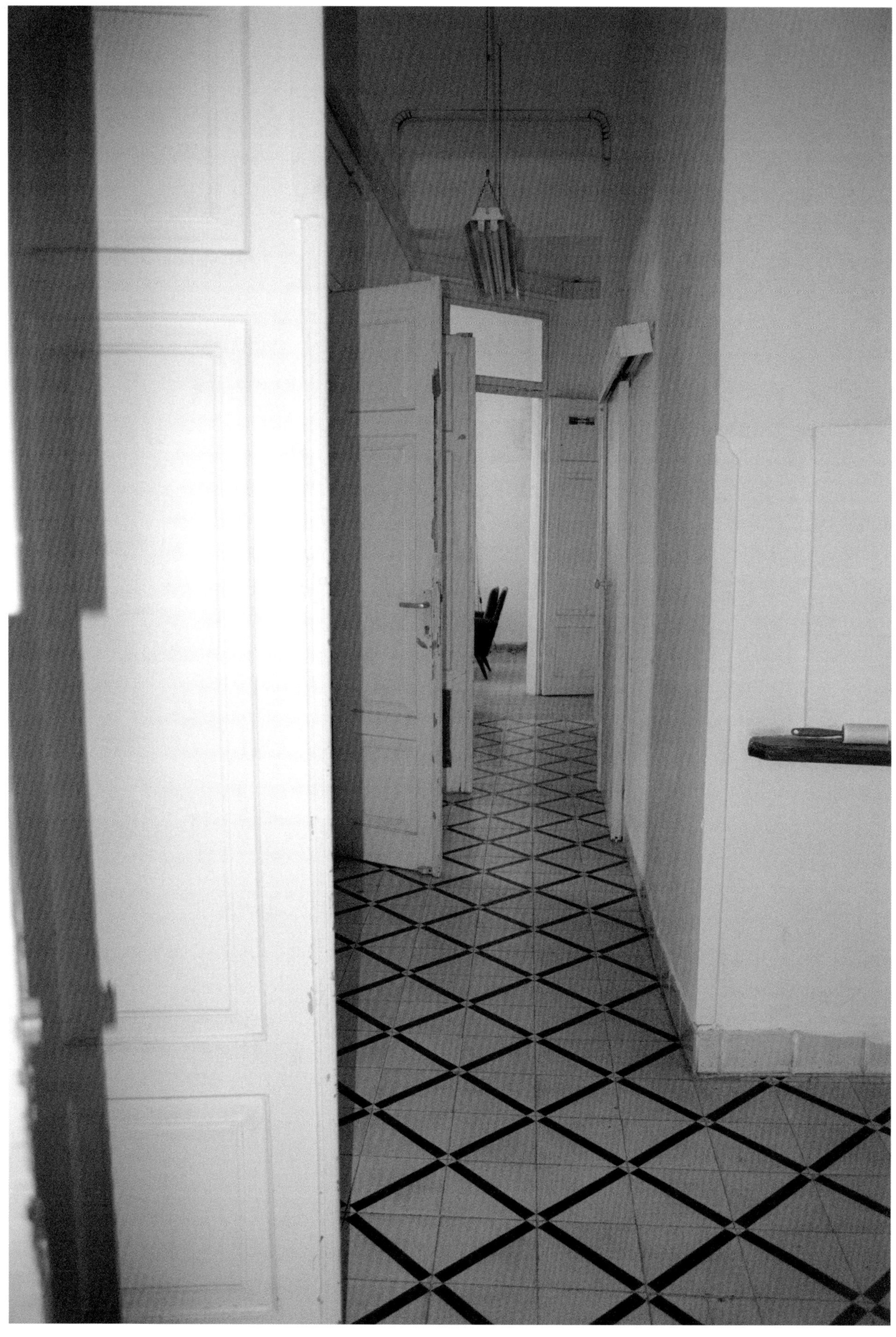

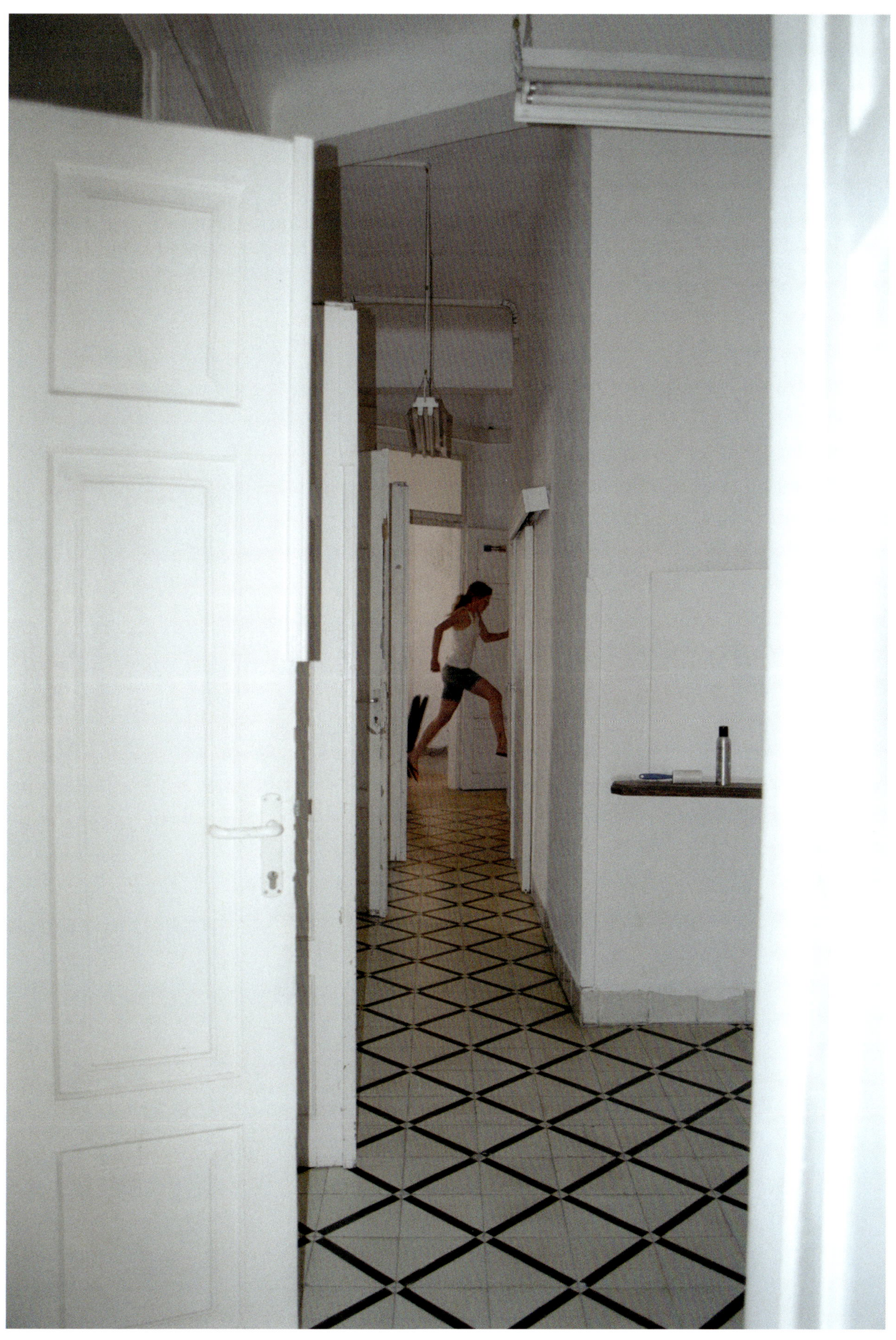

No. 3

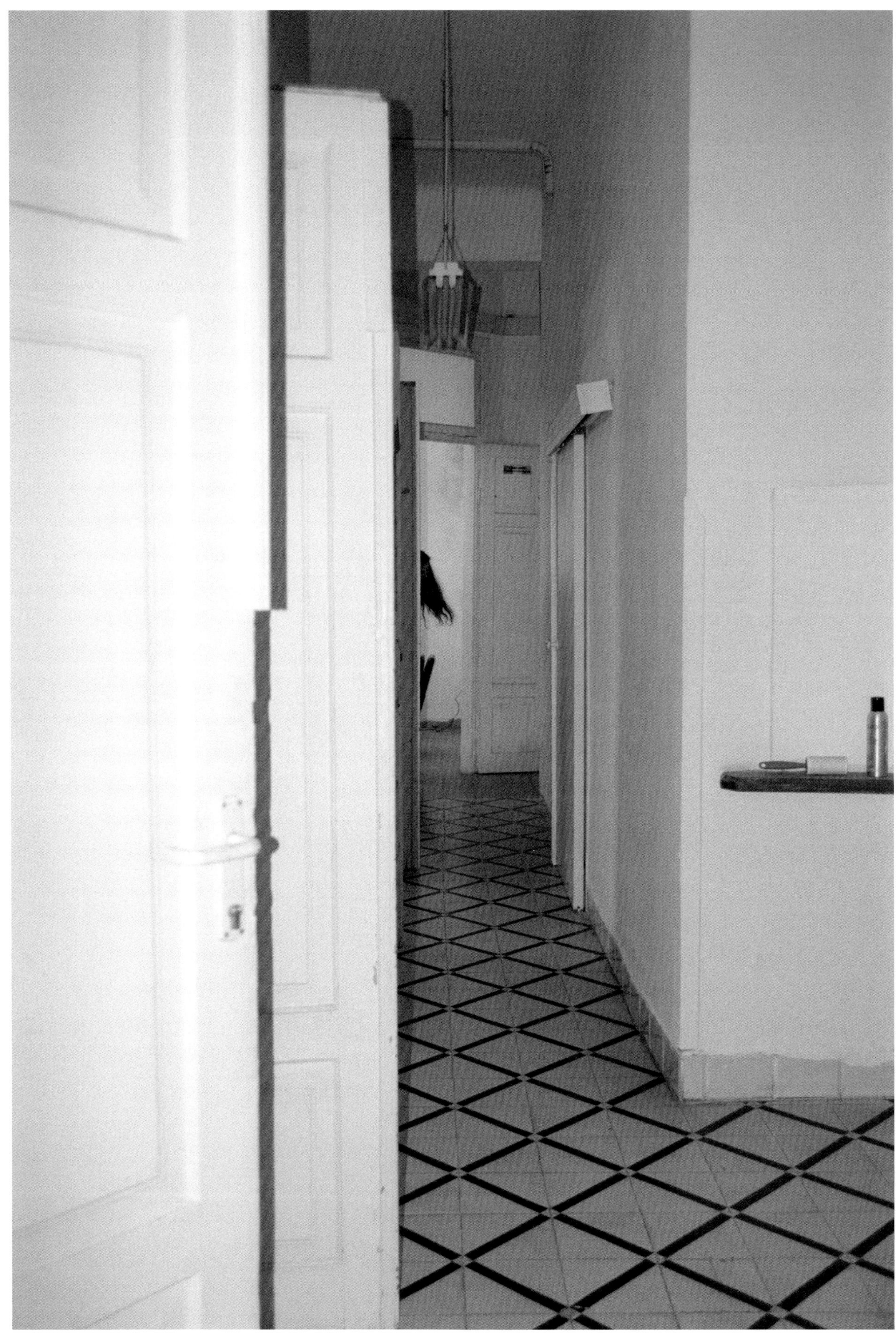

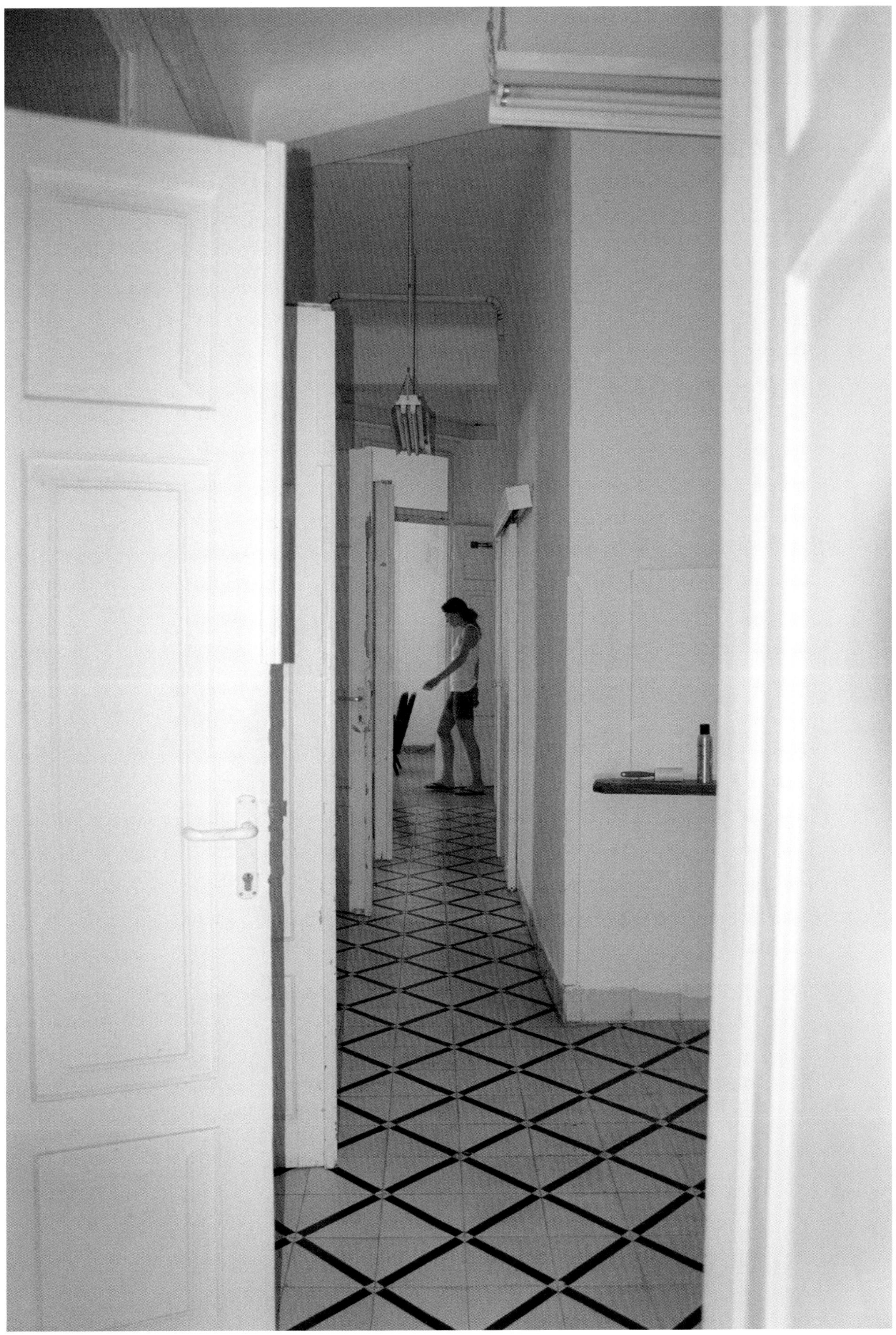

No. 12

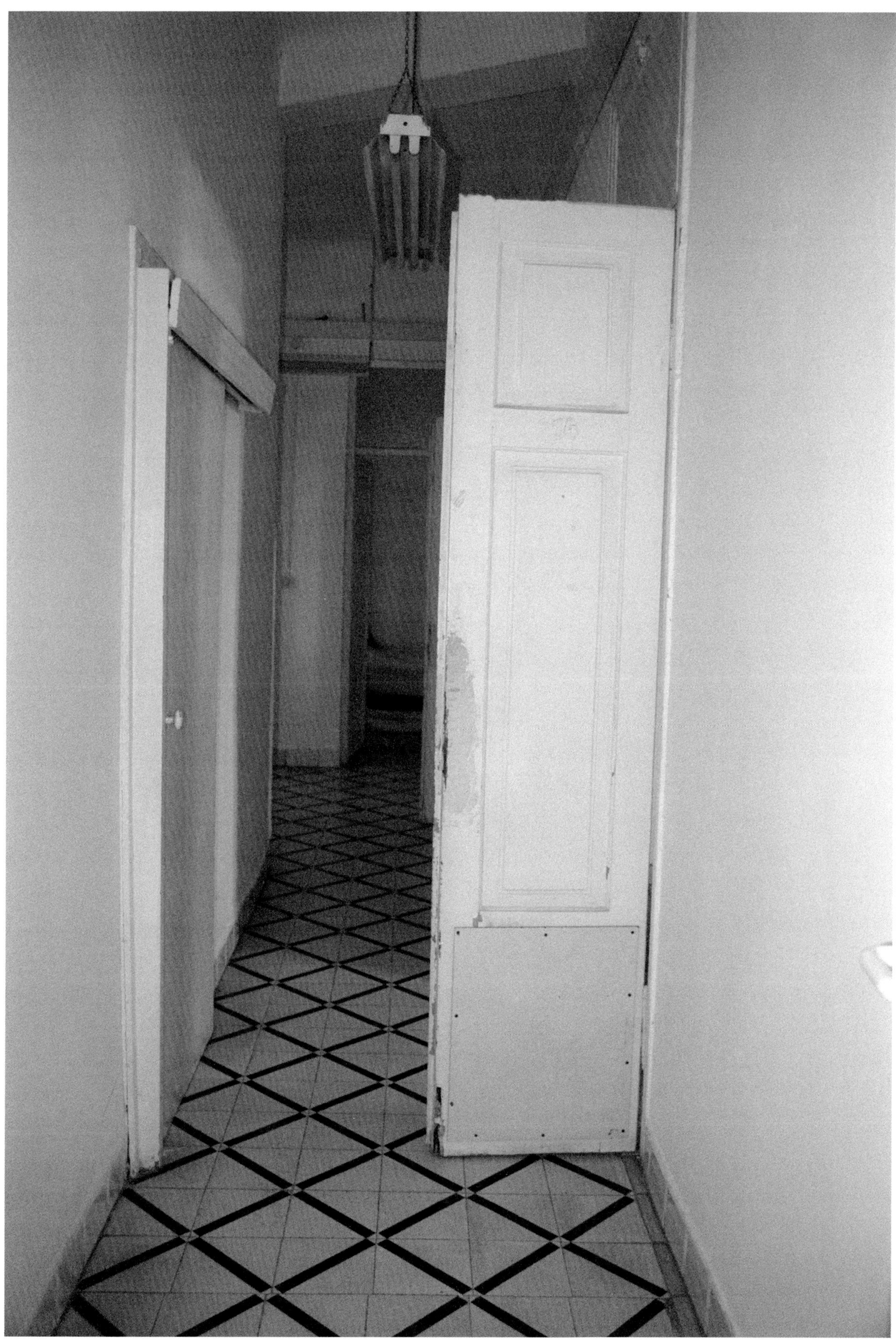

No. 14

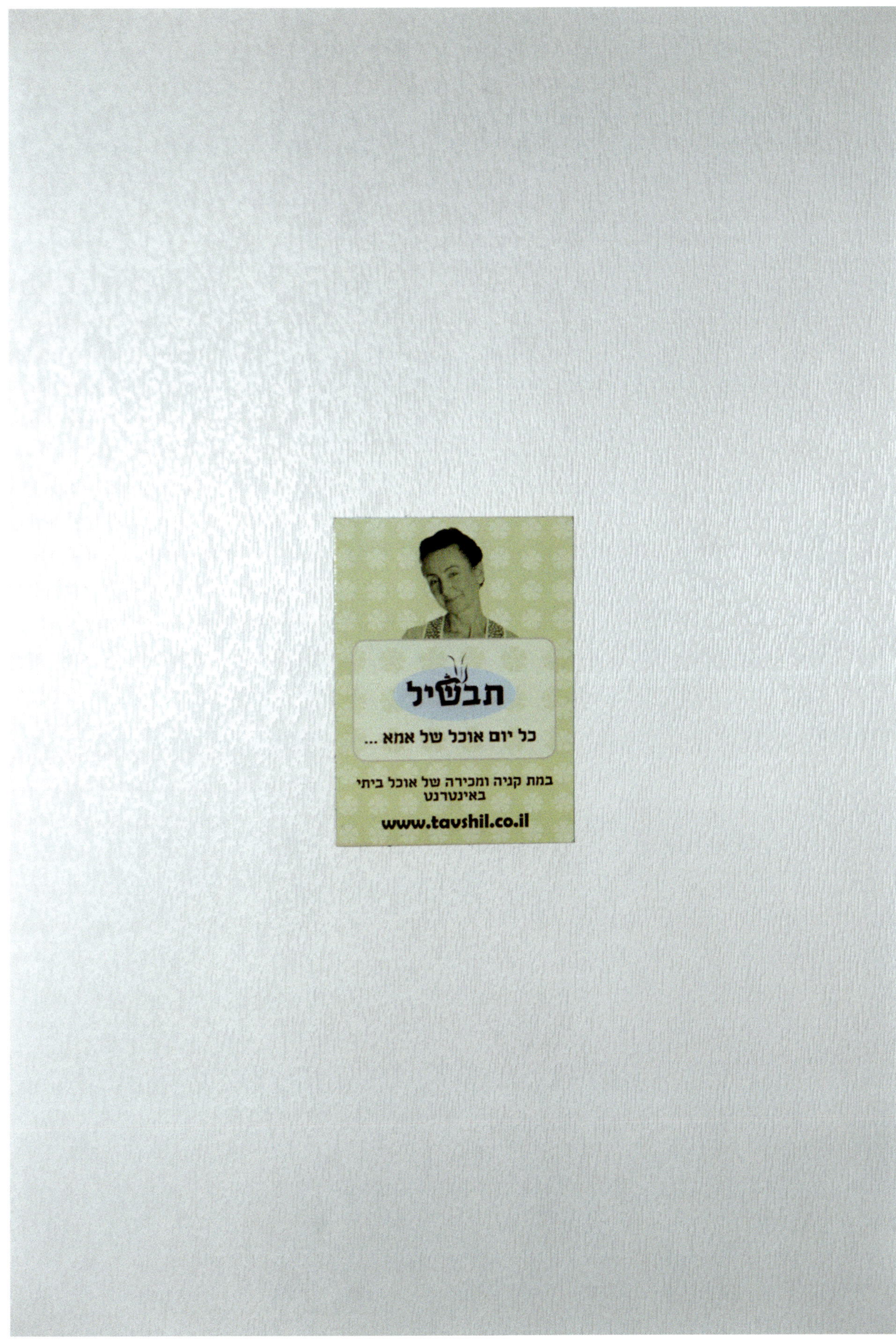
תבשיל
כל יום אוכל של אמא ...
במת קניה ומכירה של אוכל ביתי
באינטרנט
www.tavshil.co.il

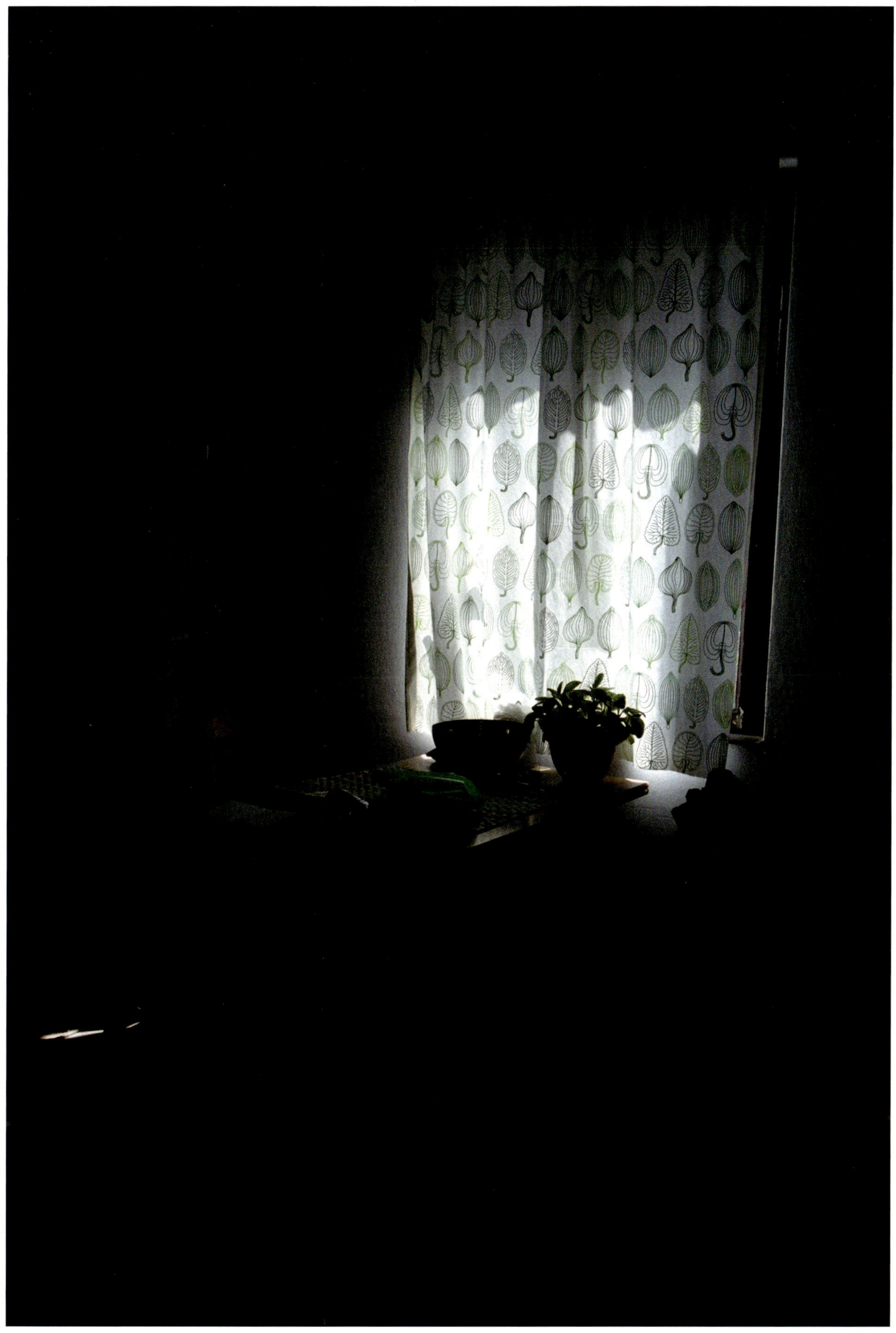

No. 6

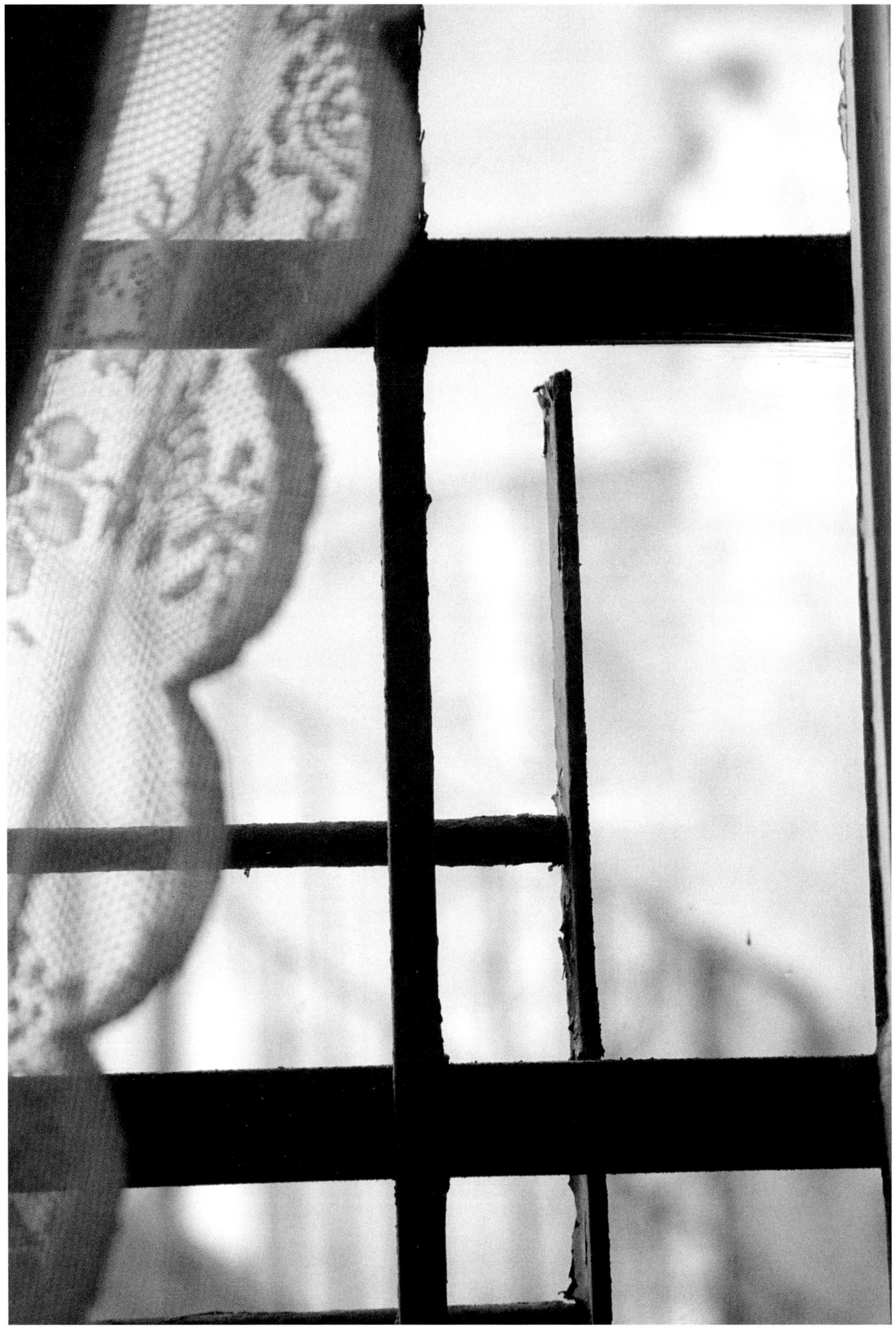

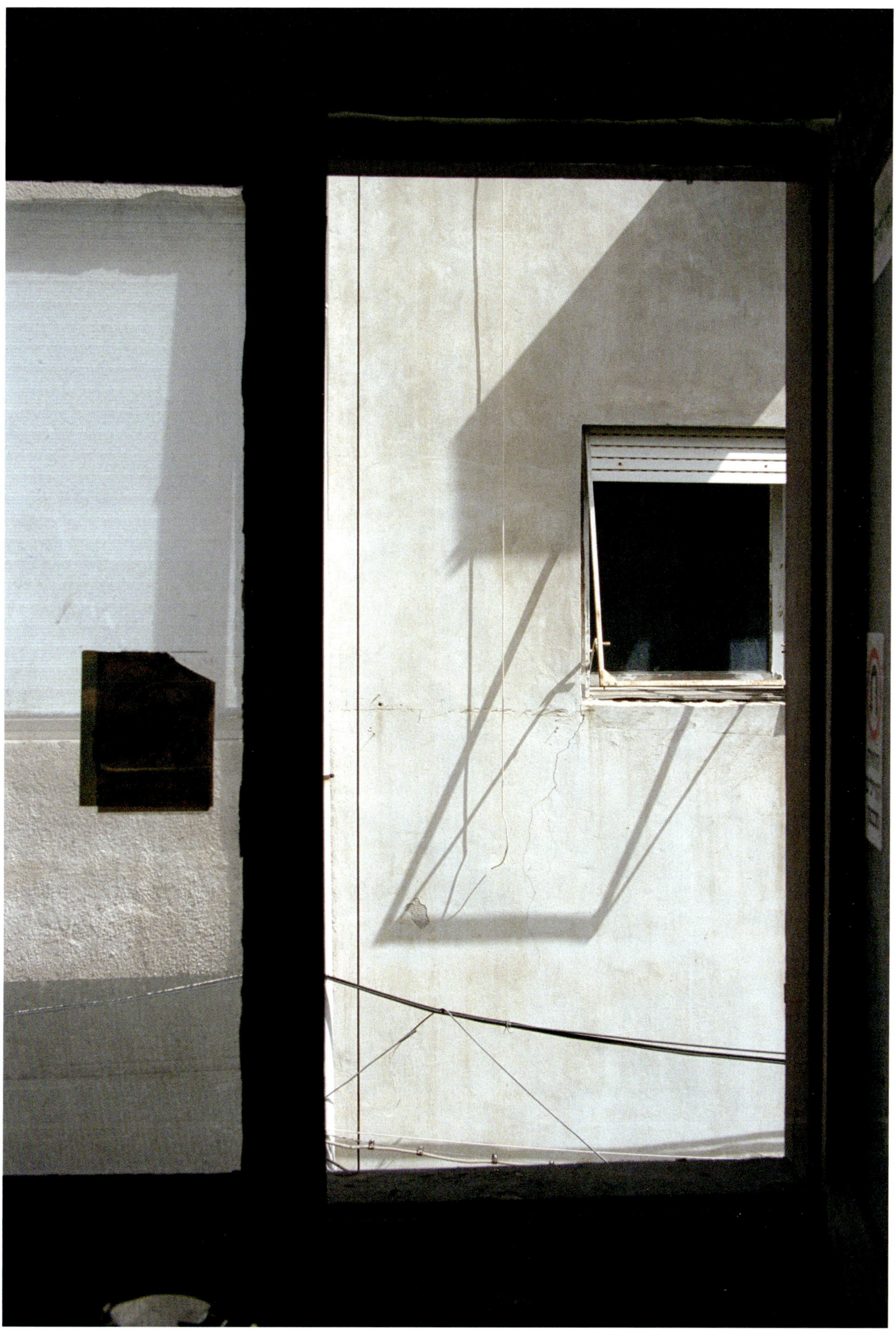

No. 21

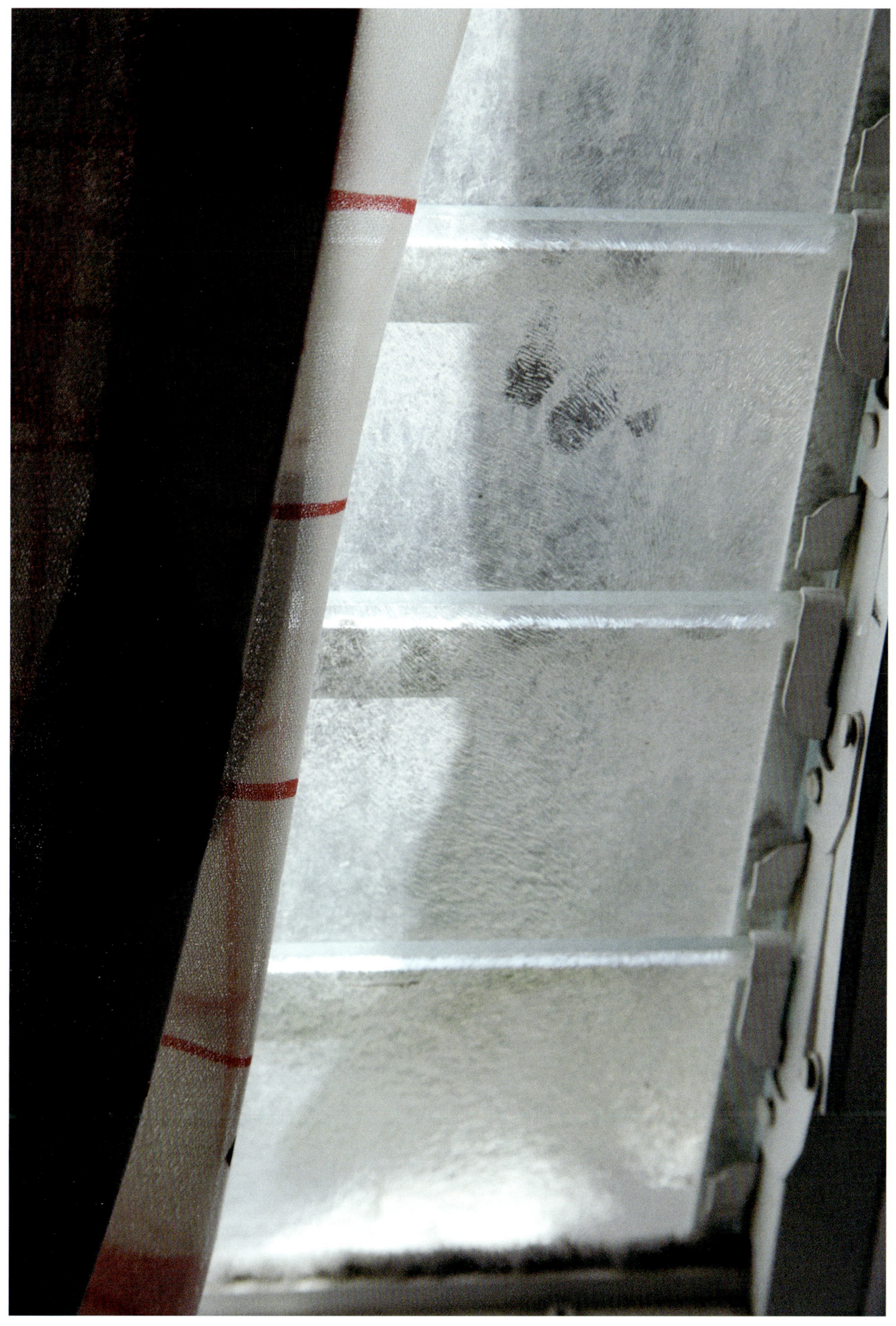

No. 25

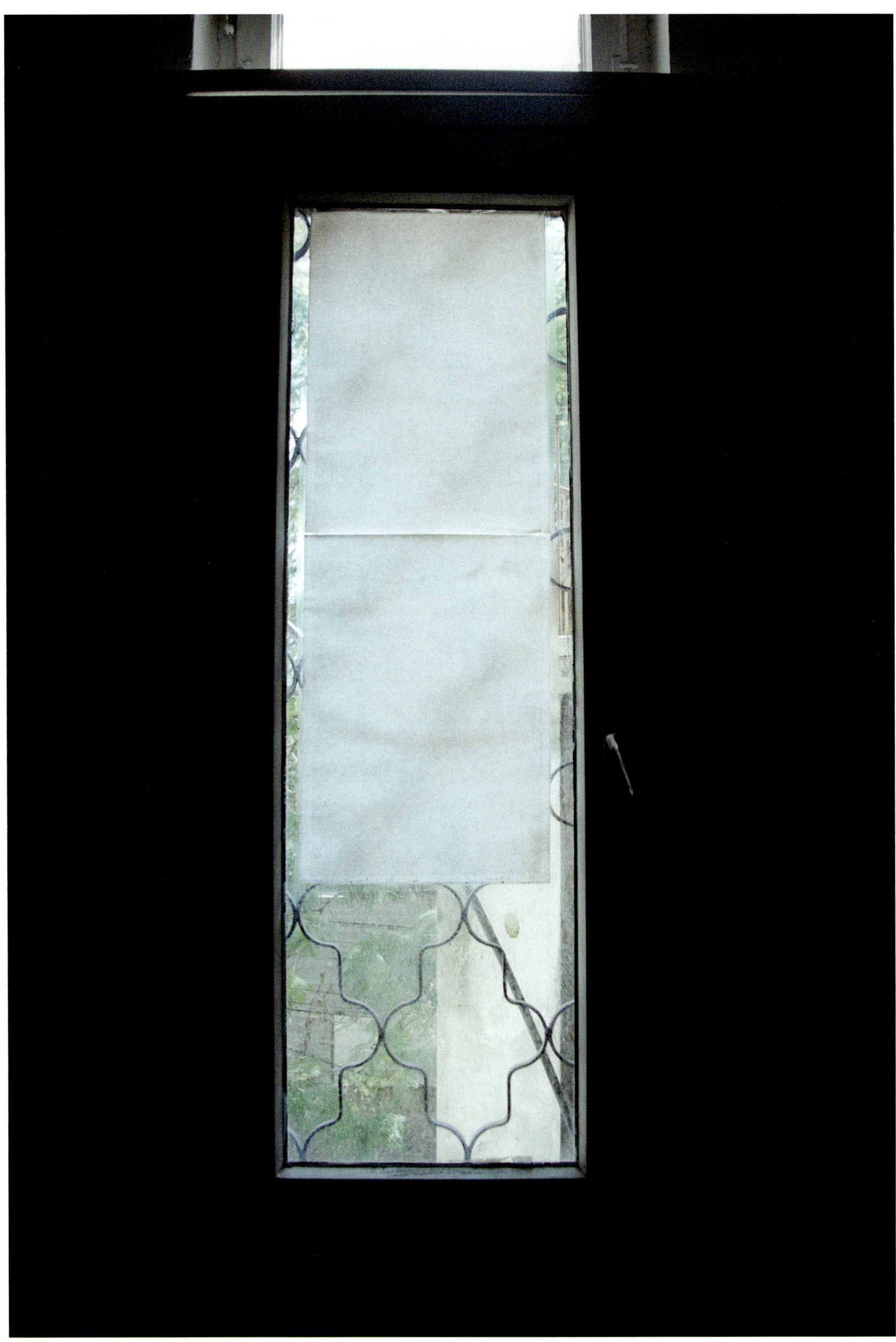



No. 23

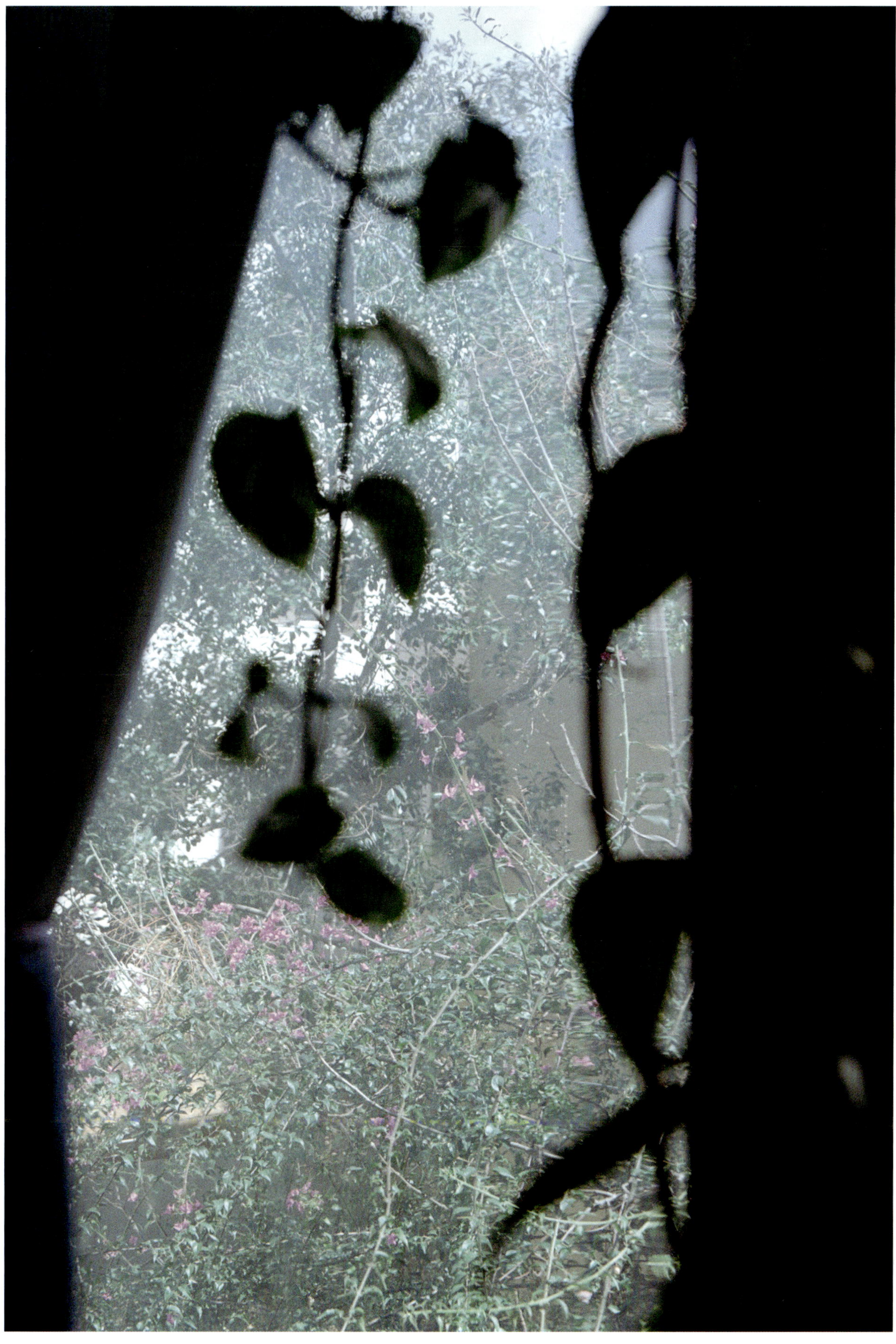

No. 22

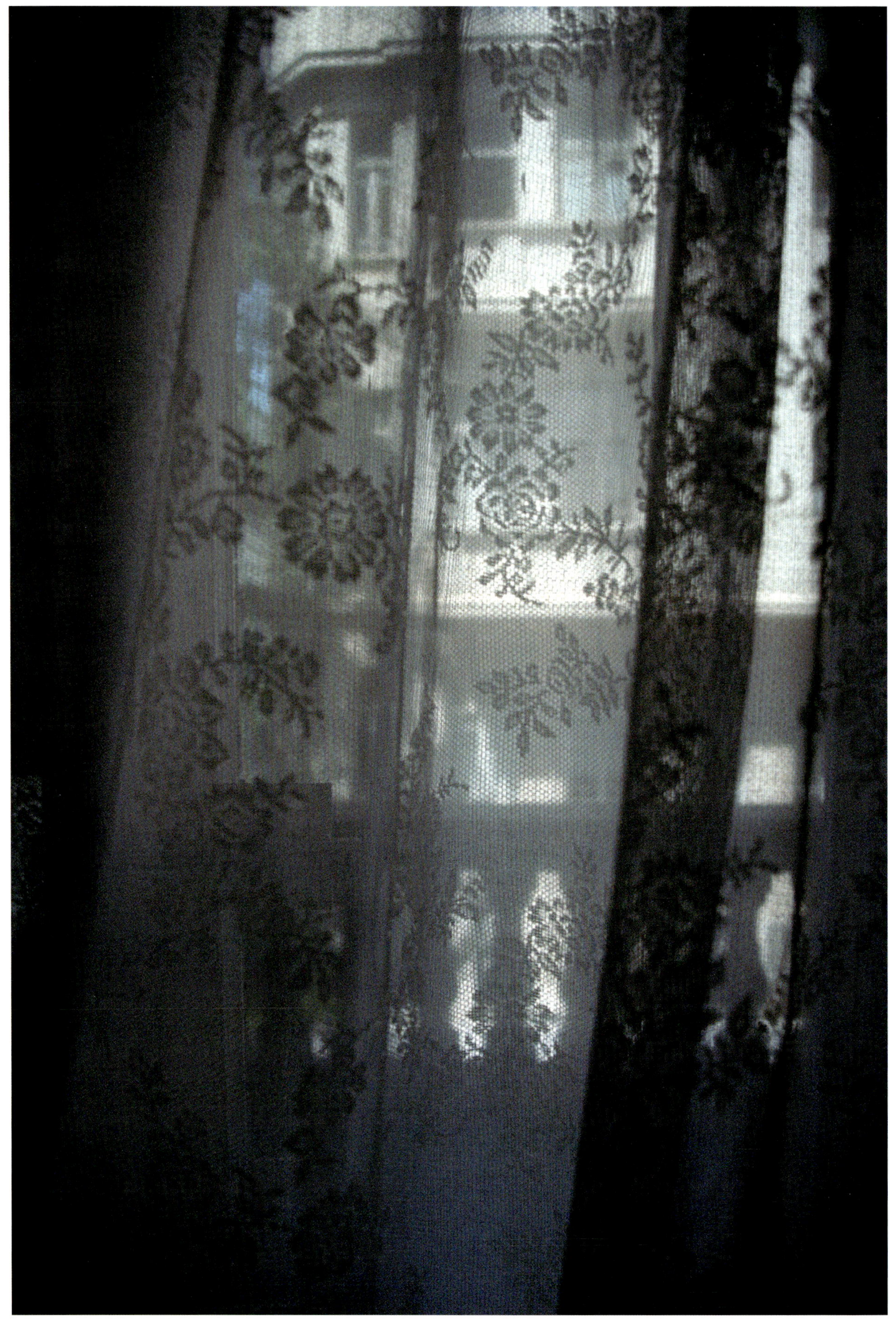



No. 5

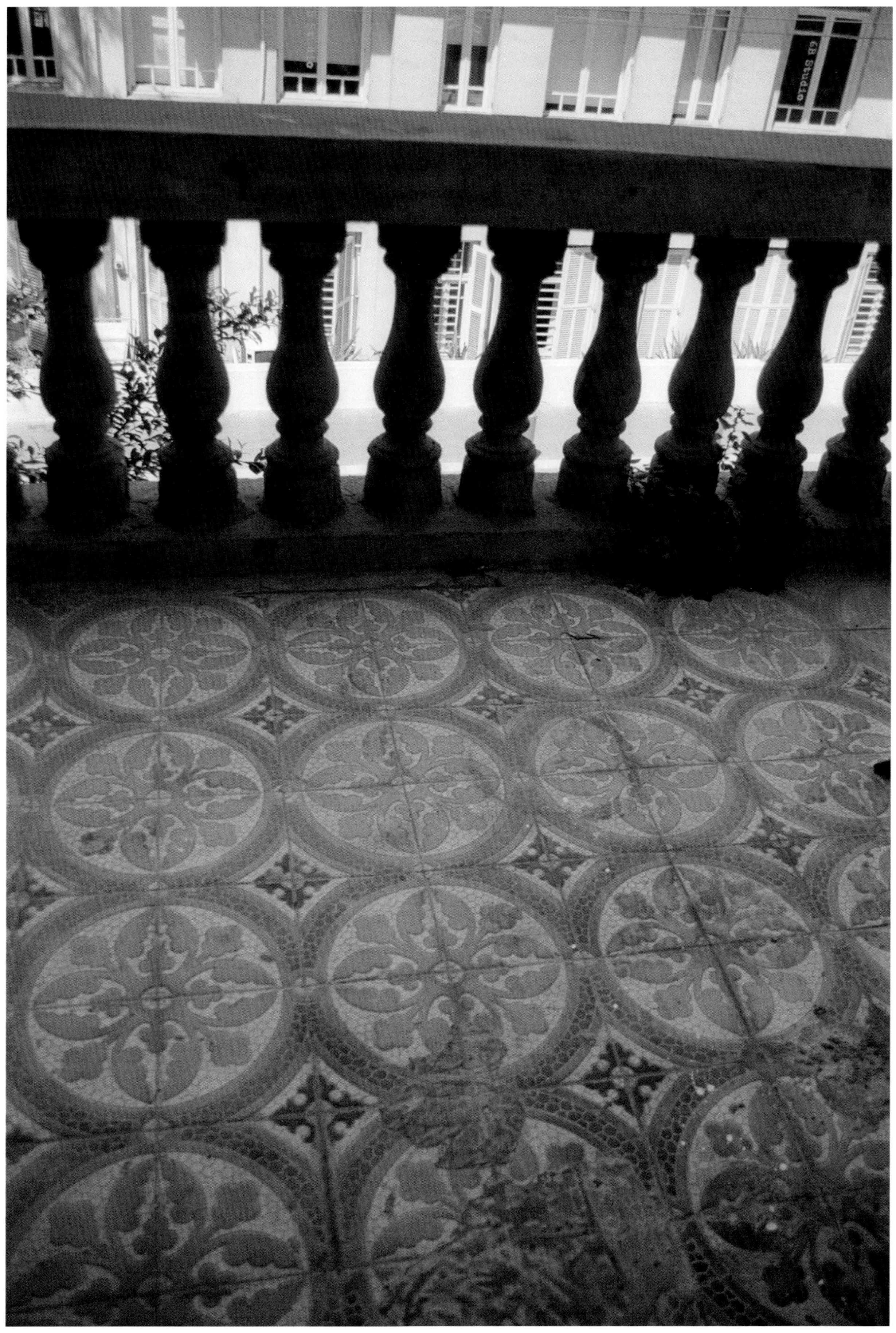

No. 17

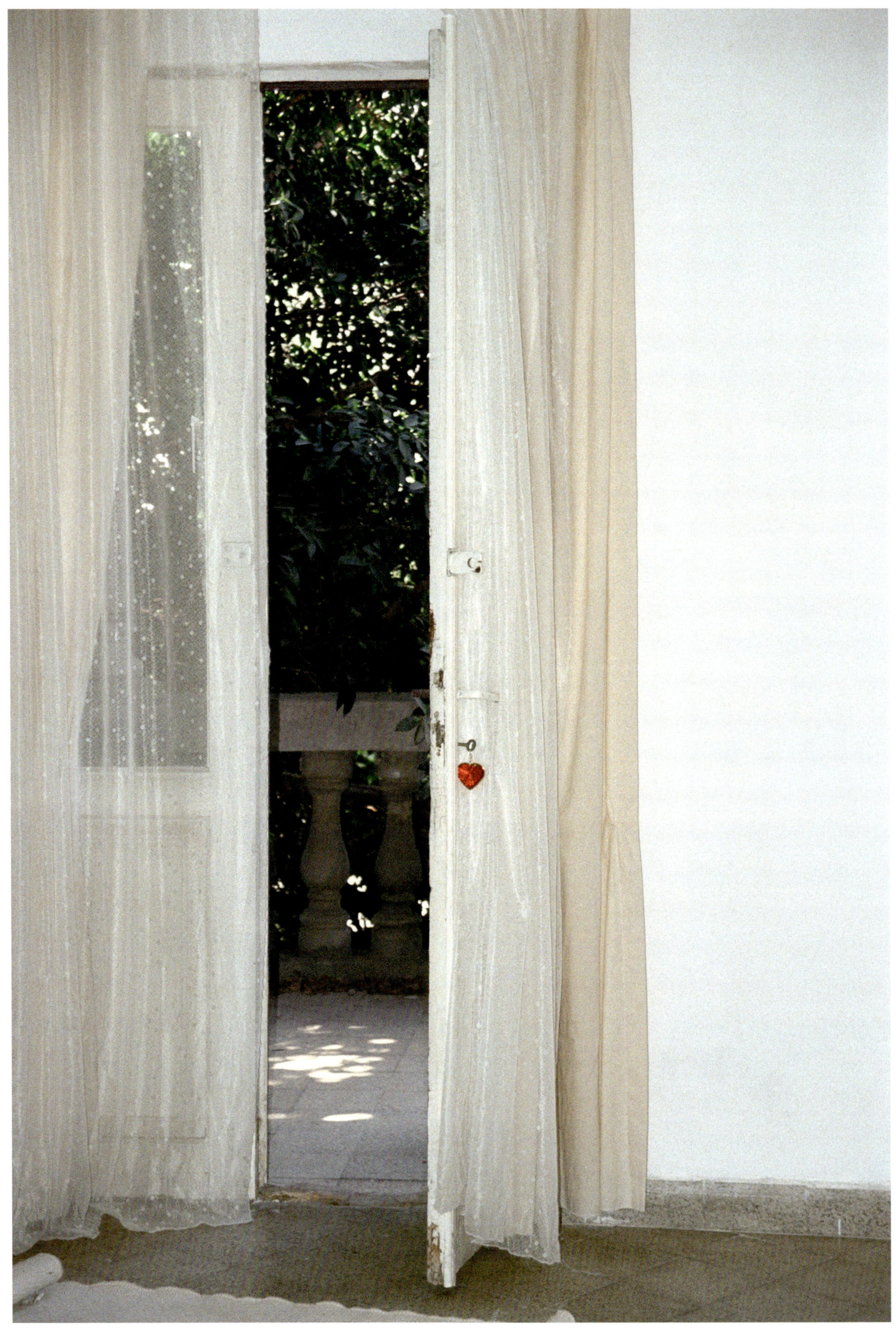



No. 16

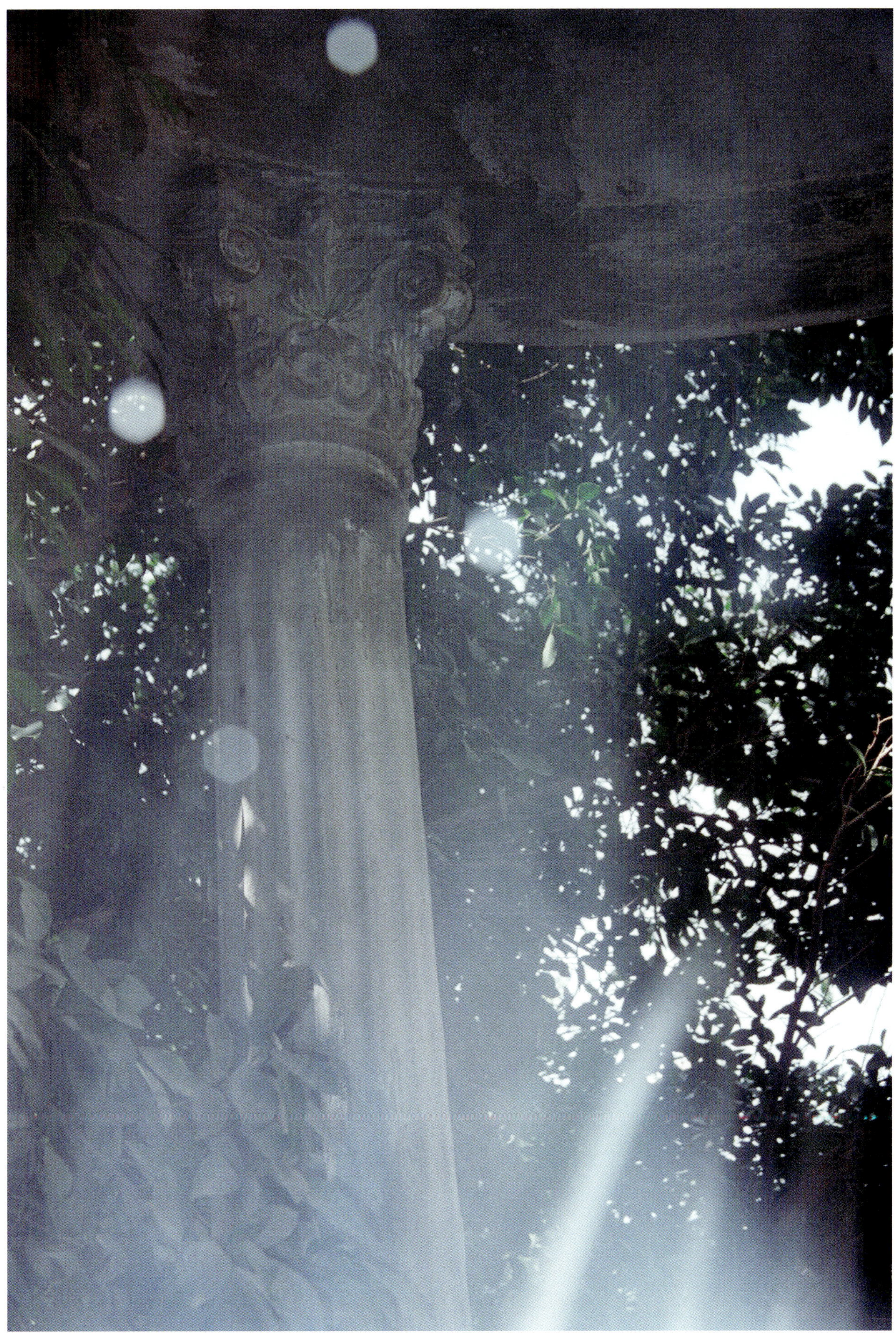

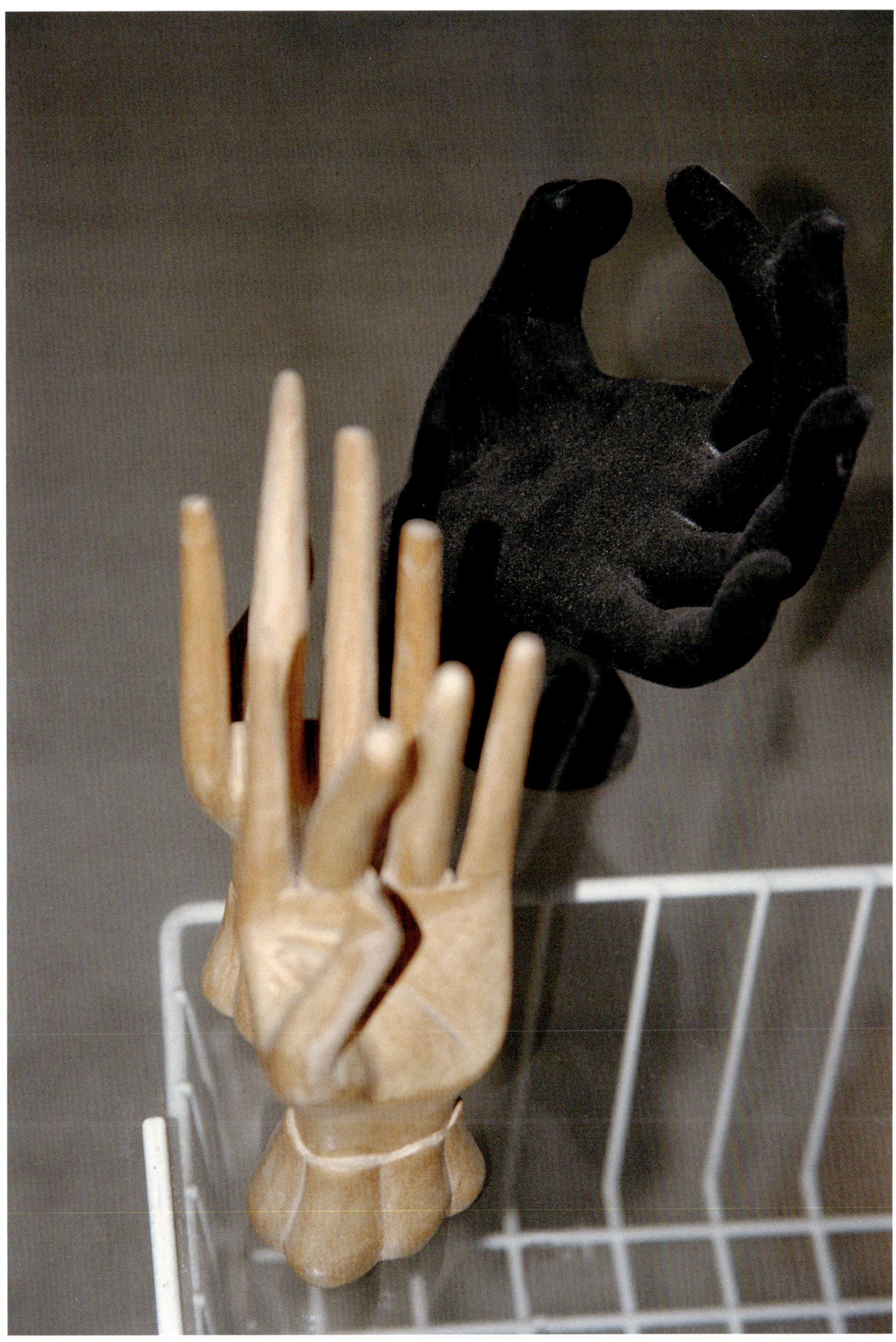

No. E1

# Drawings

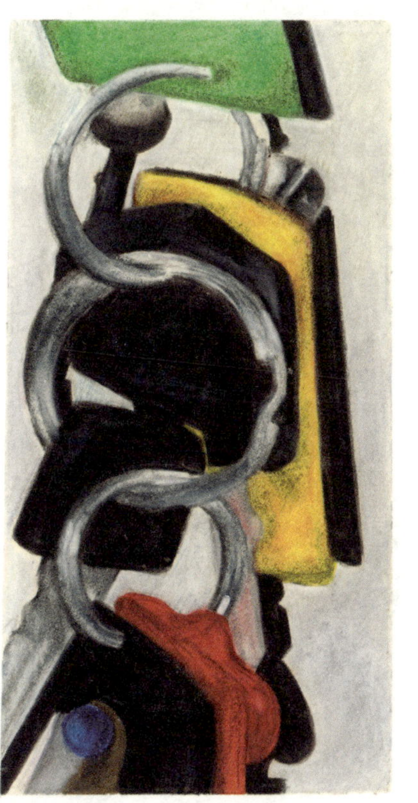

I

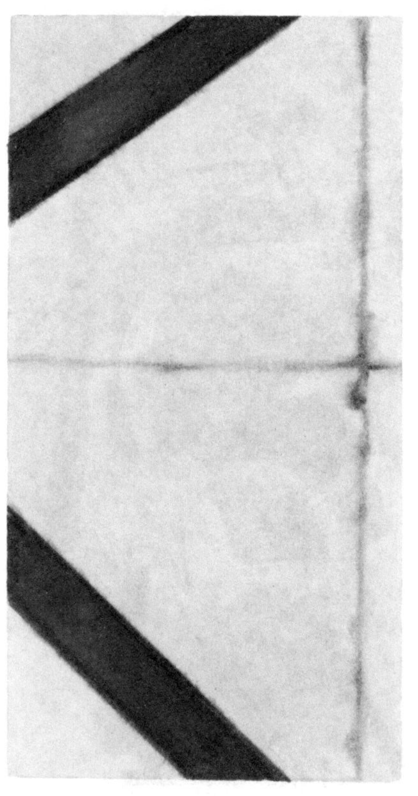

II

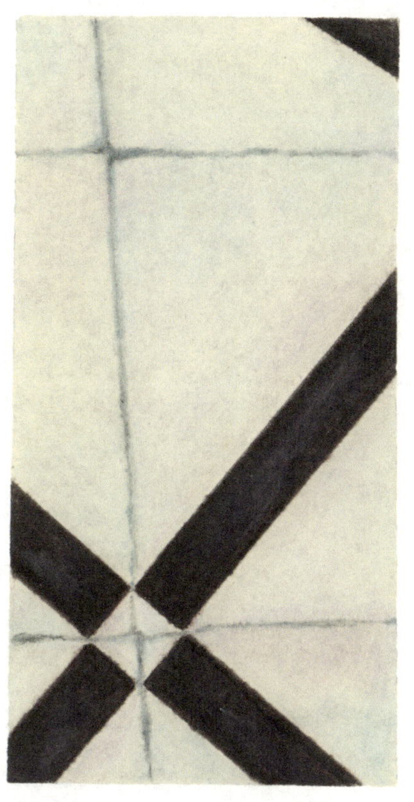

III

IV

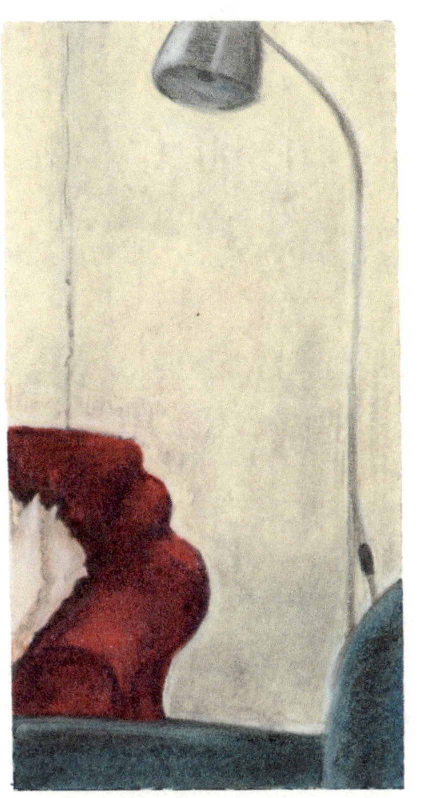

V

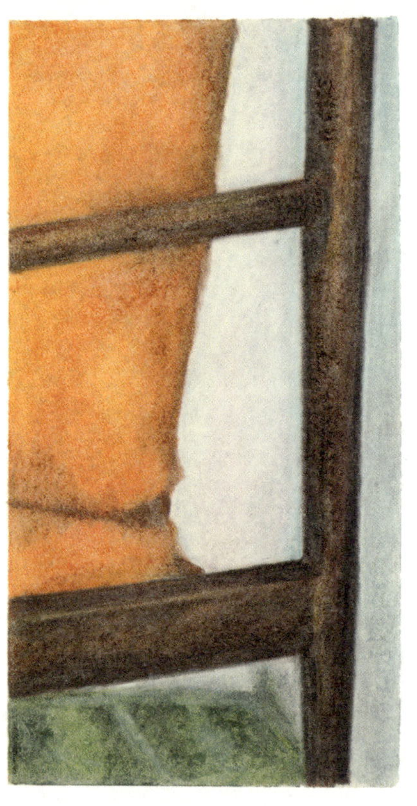

VI

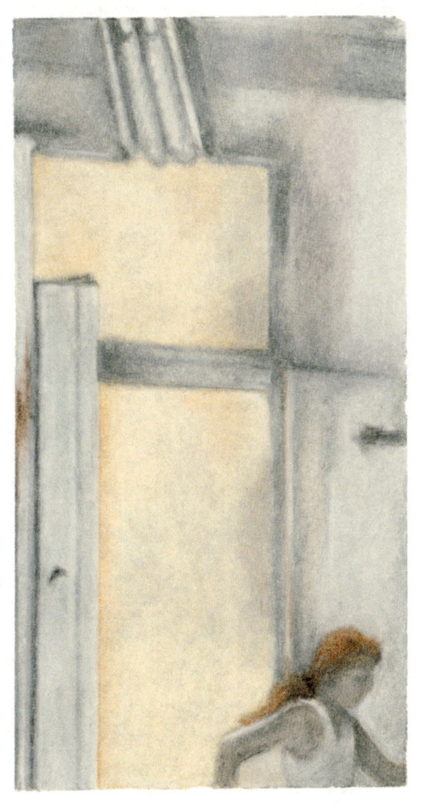

VII

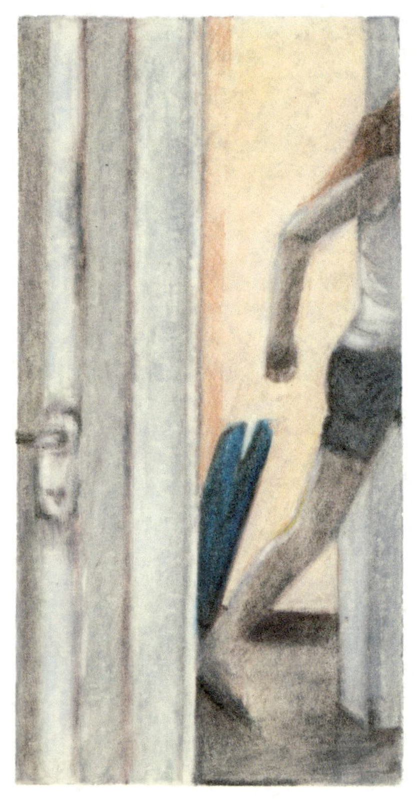

VIII

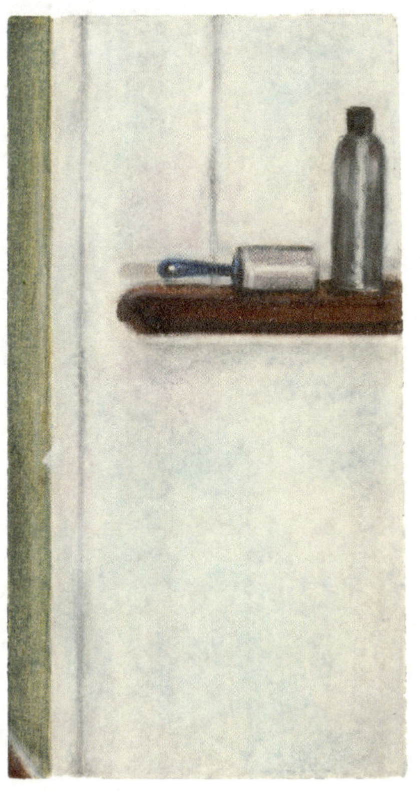

IX

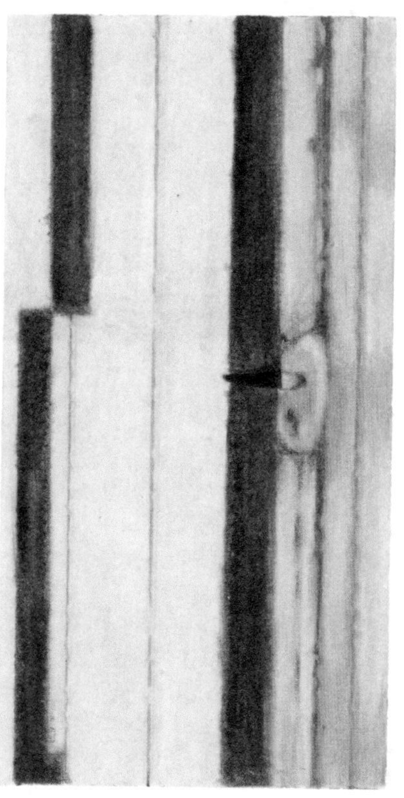

X

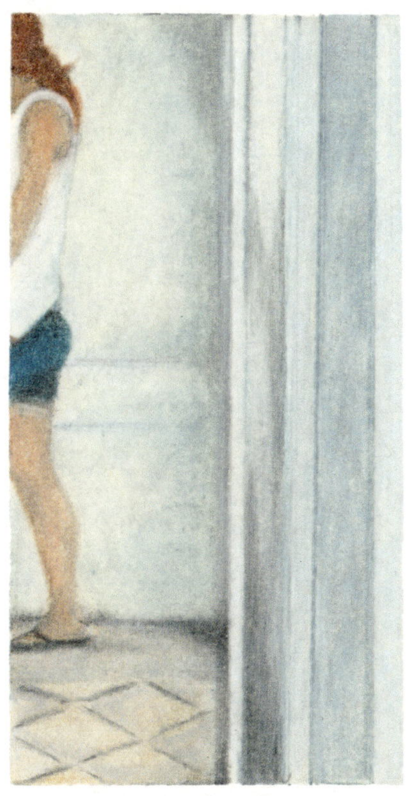

XI

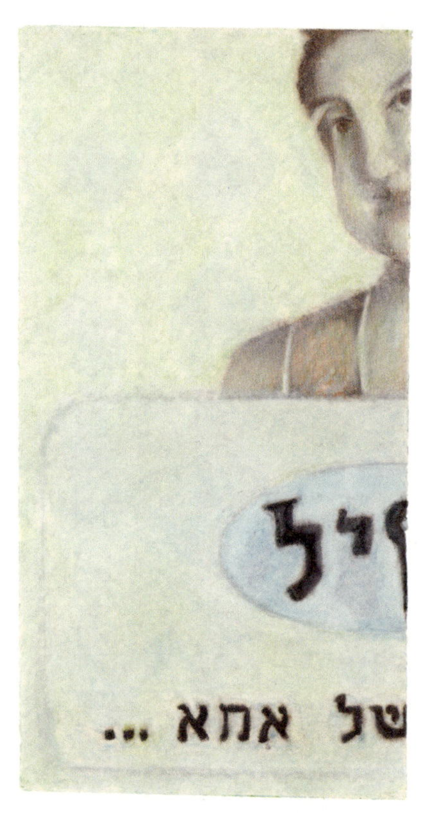
יל
ל אתא ...

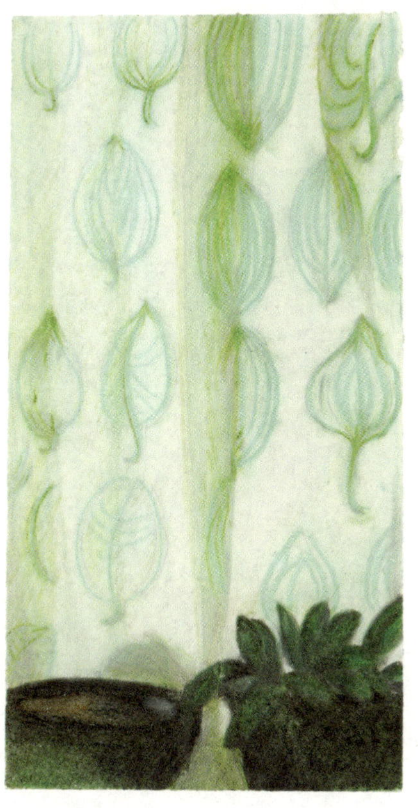

XIII

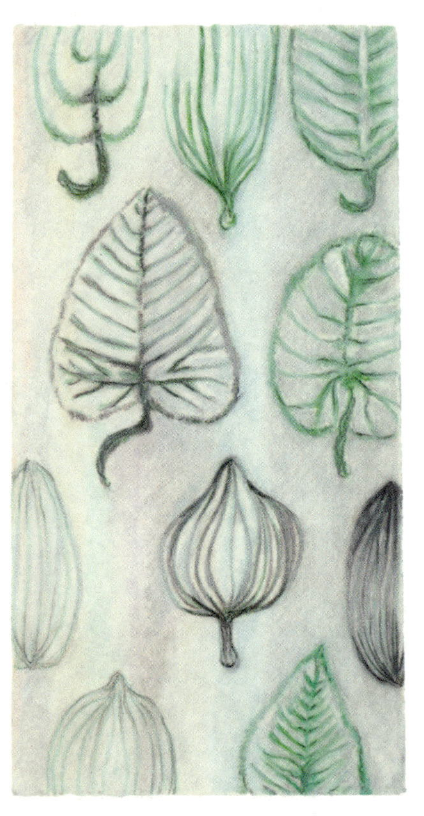

XIV

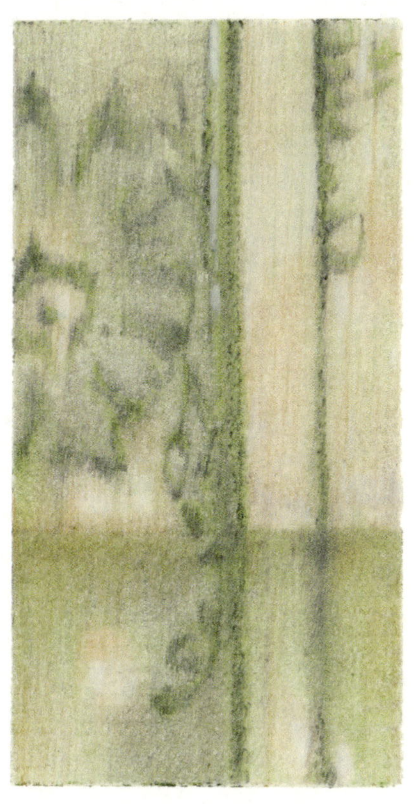

XV

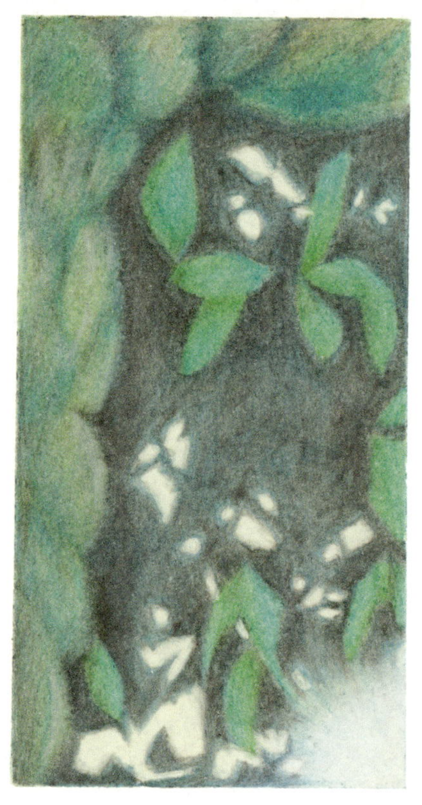

XVI

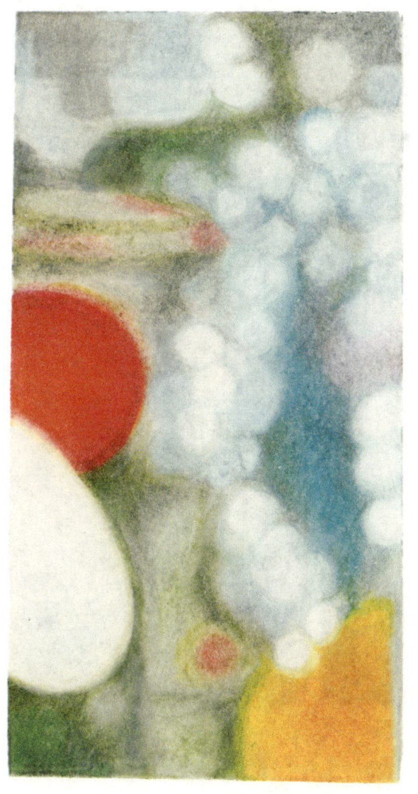

XVII

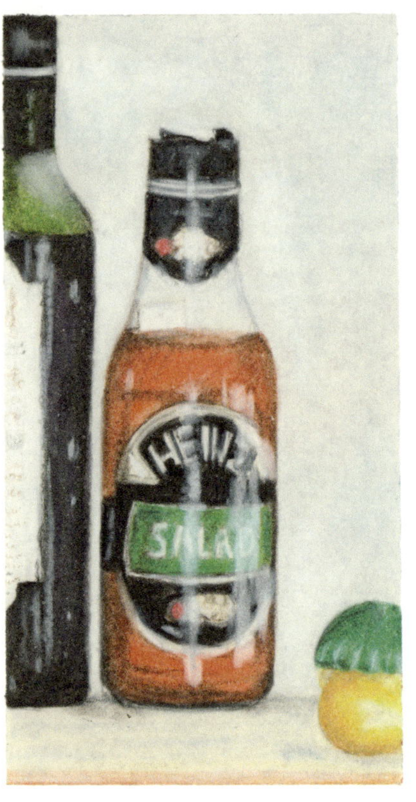


XVIII

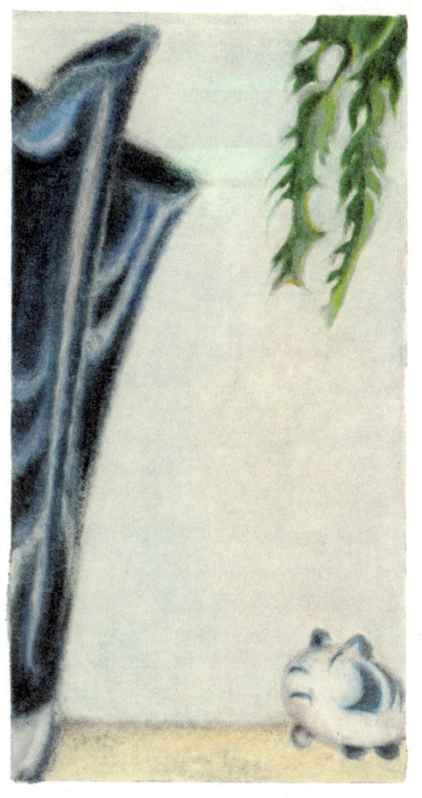

XIX

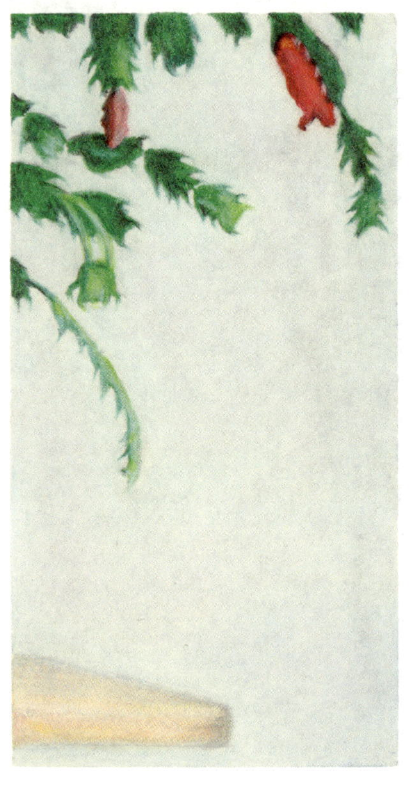

XX

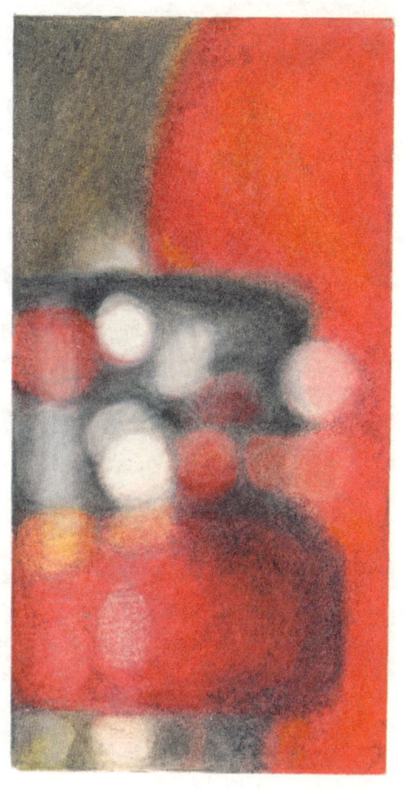

XXI

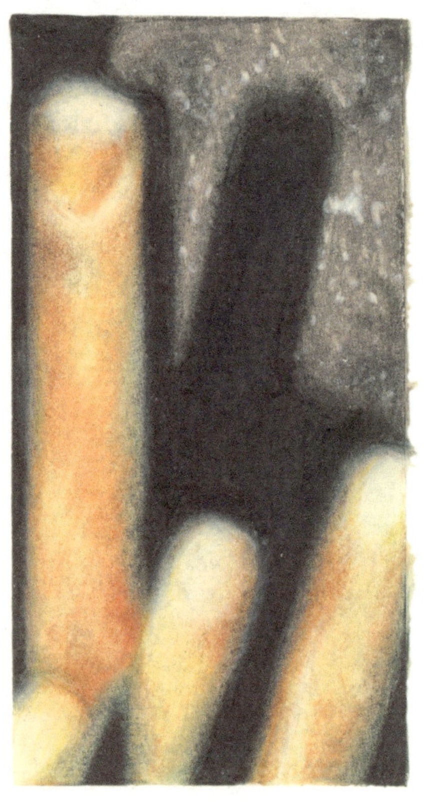

XXII

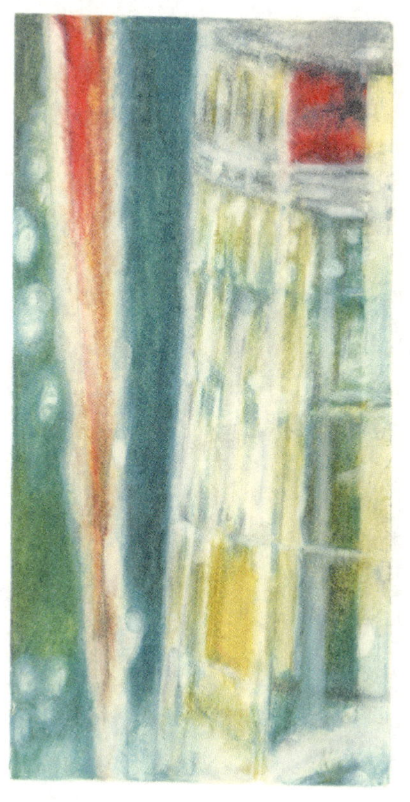

XXIII

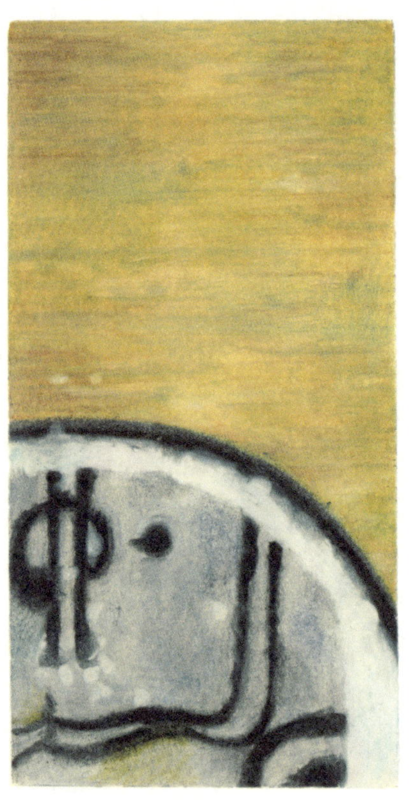

XXIV

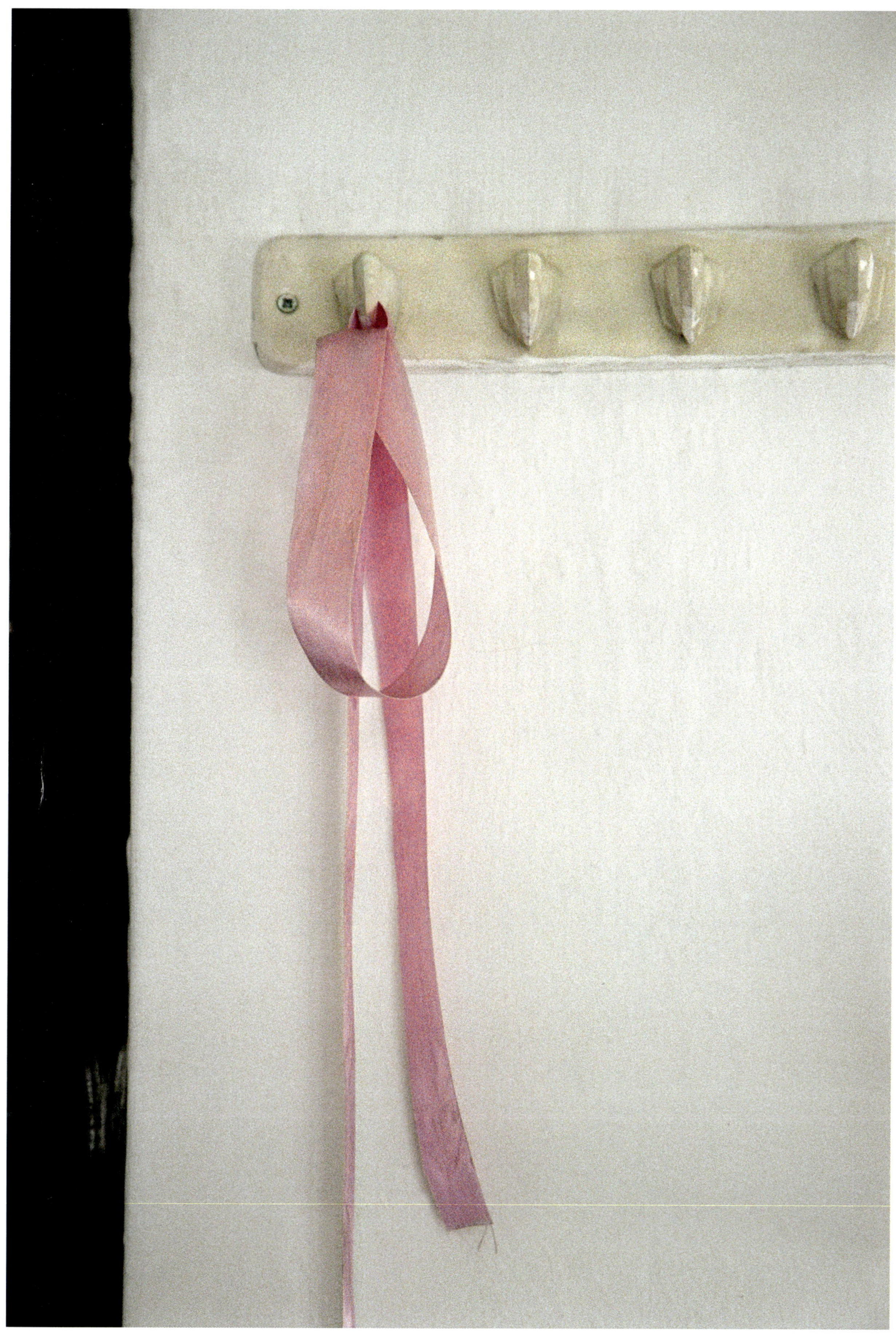

No. E2

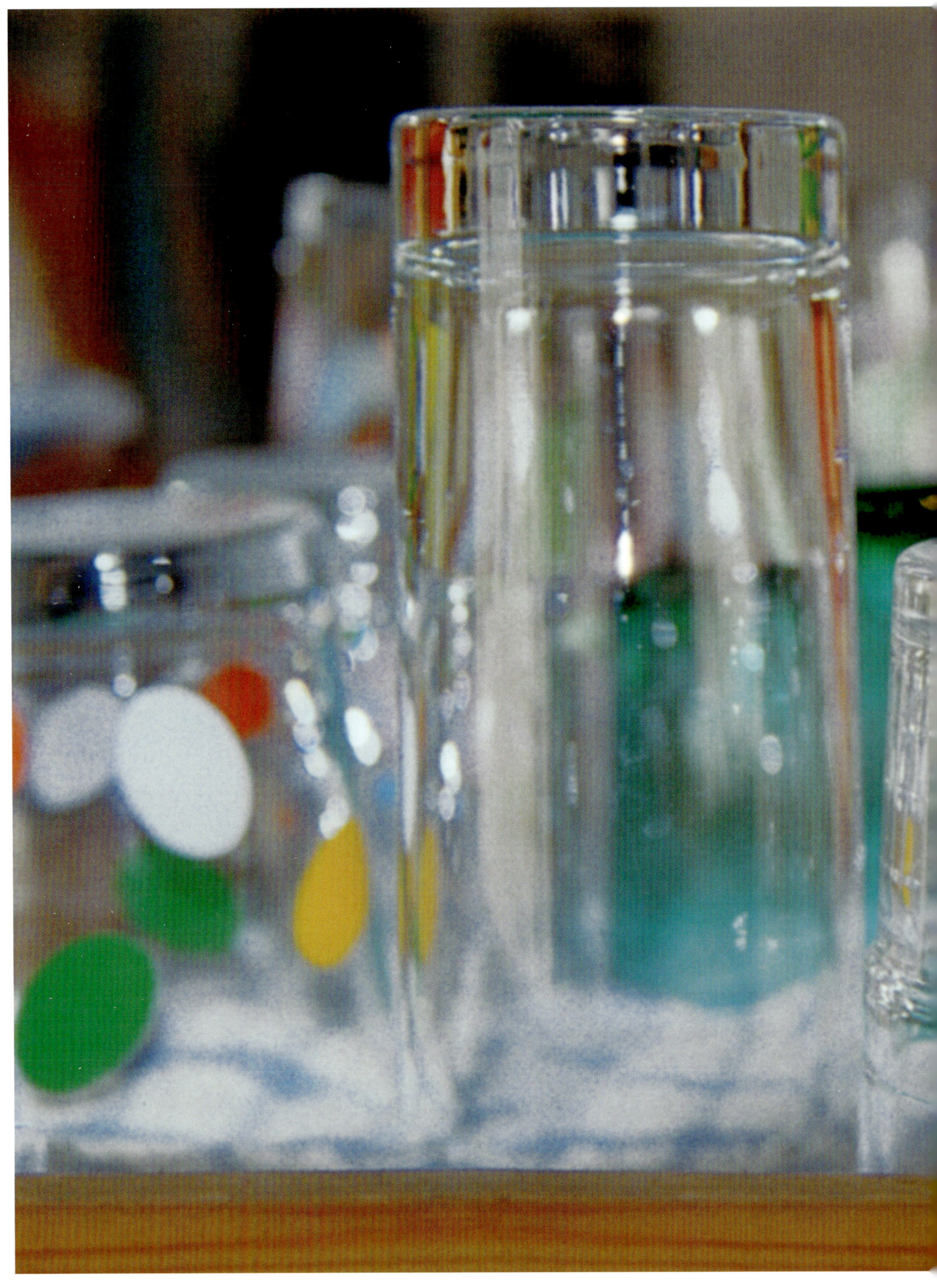



No. E3

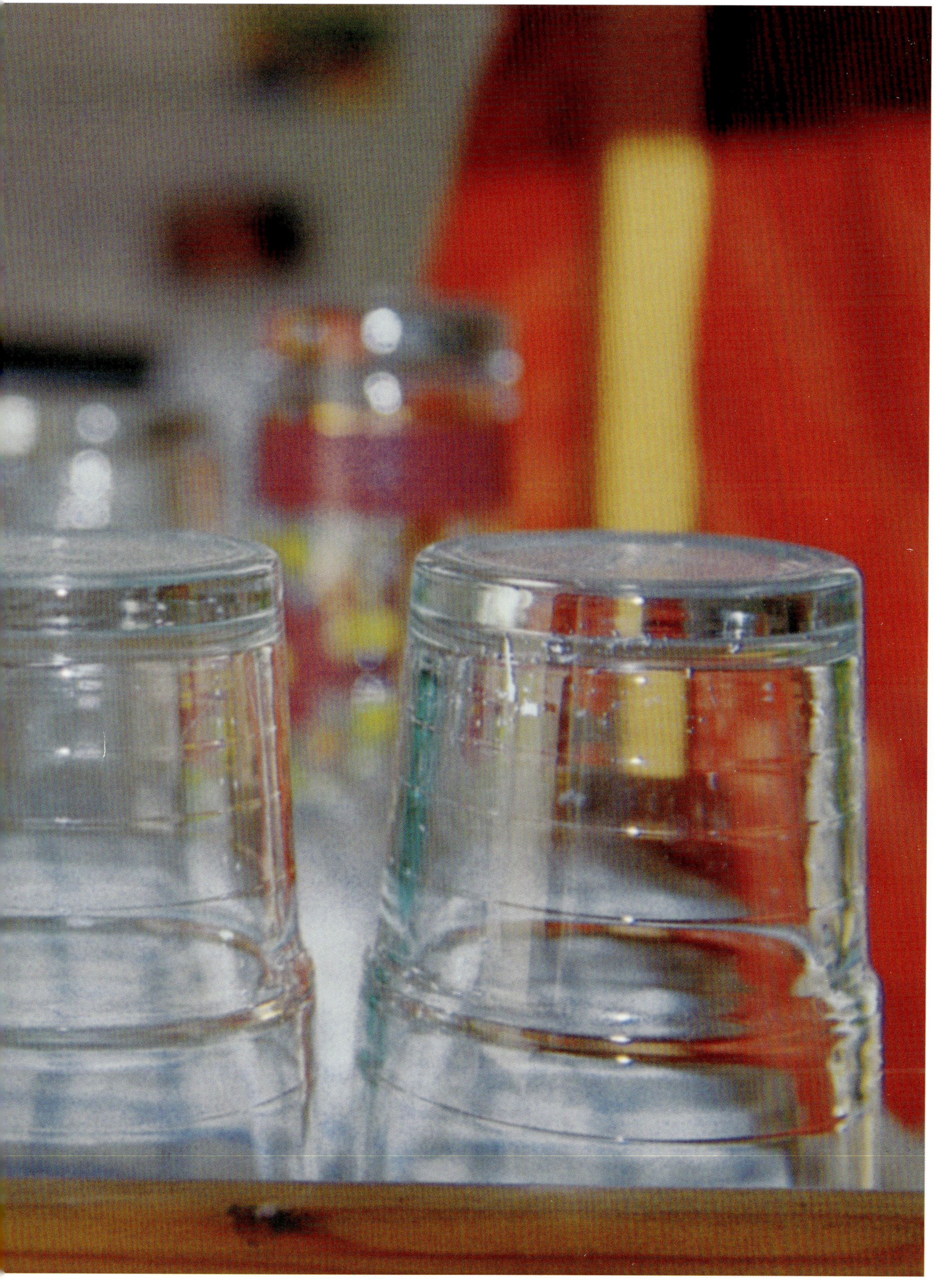

Gourmet
SALAD
VINEGAR
Aceto
Balsamico
HEINZ
Gourmet
SALAD
VINEGAR

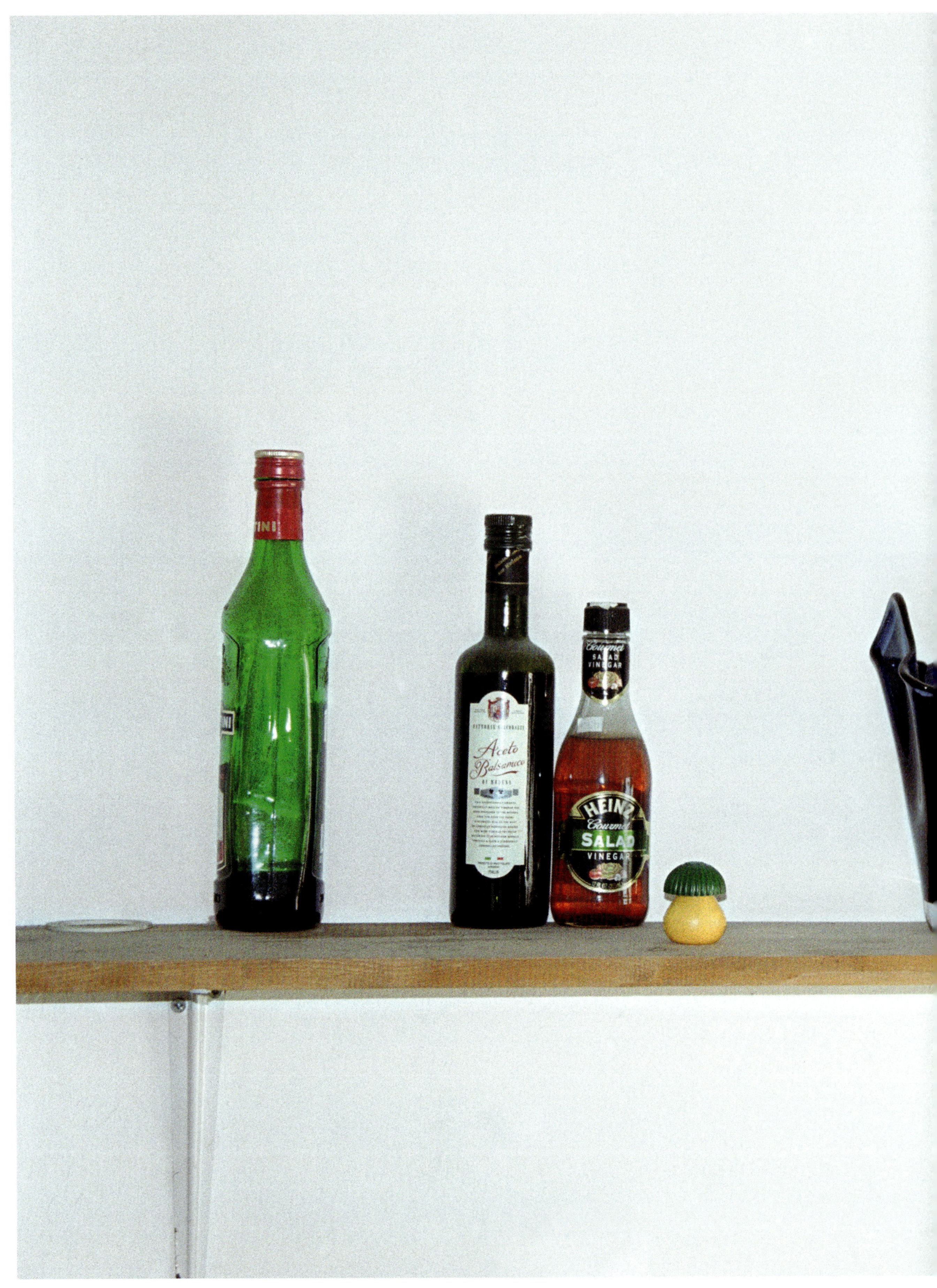

No. E4

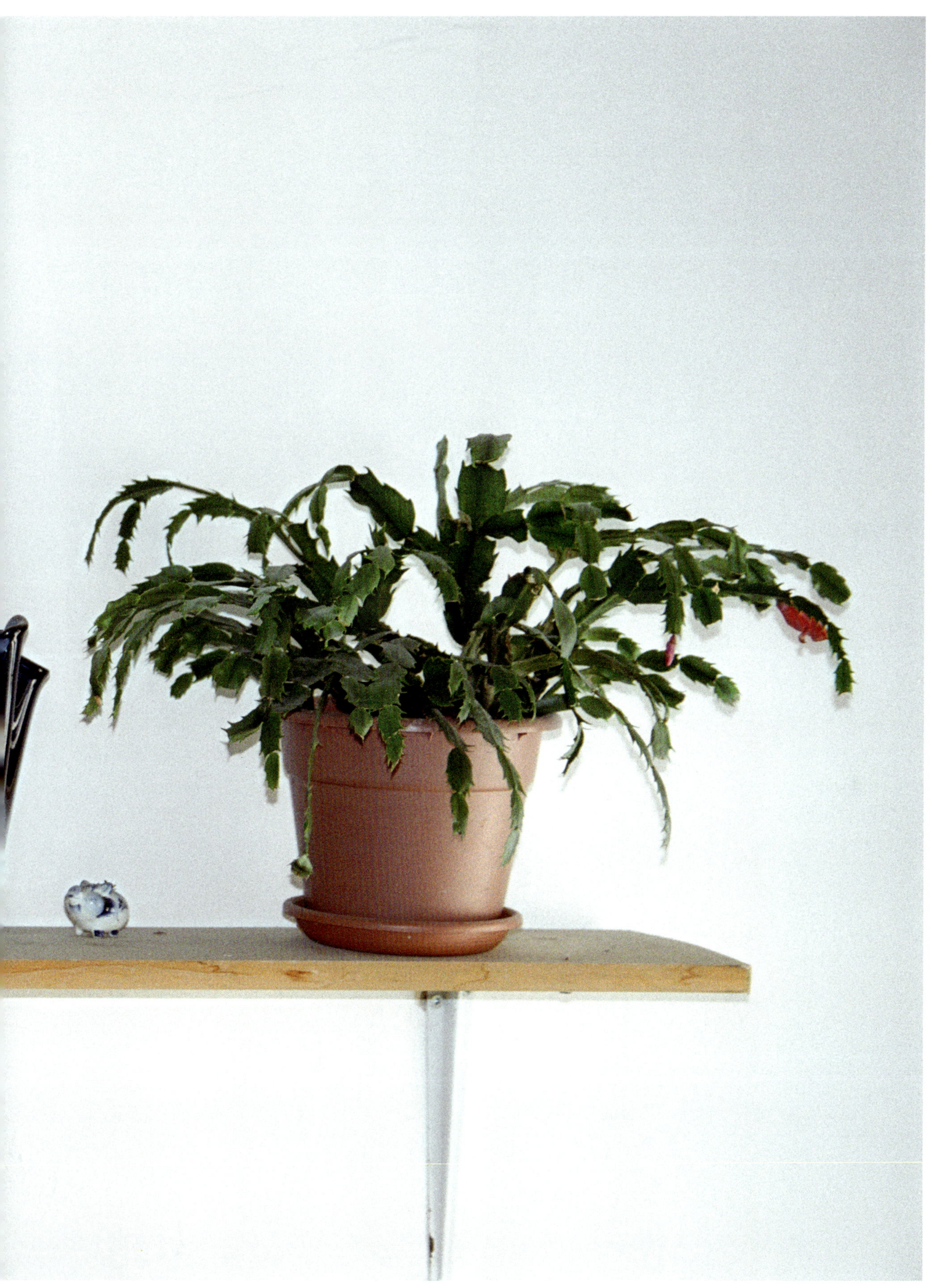

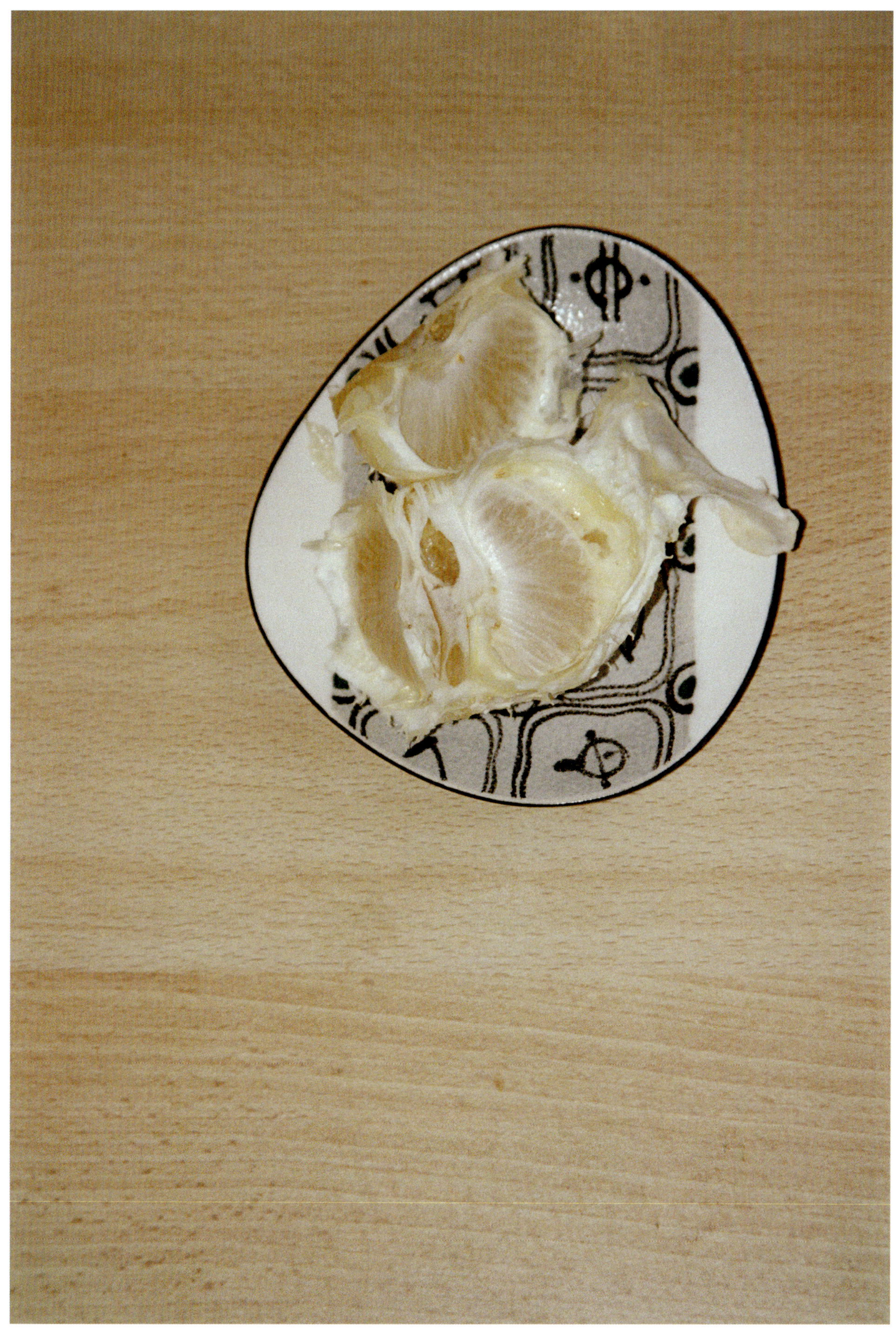

No. E5

# 53rd Venice Biennale, Arsenale

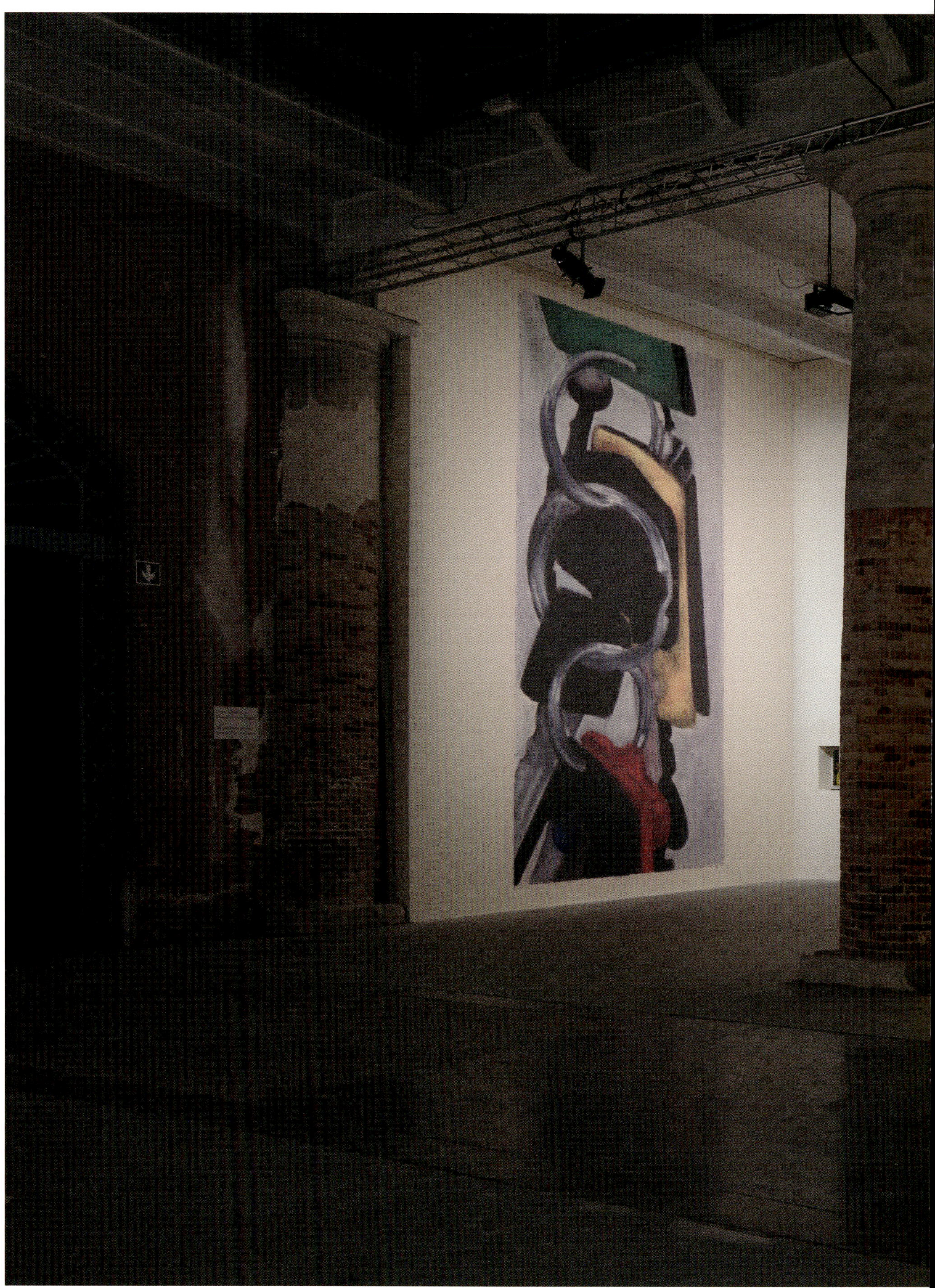

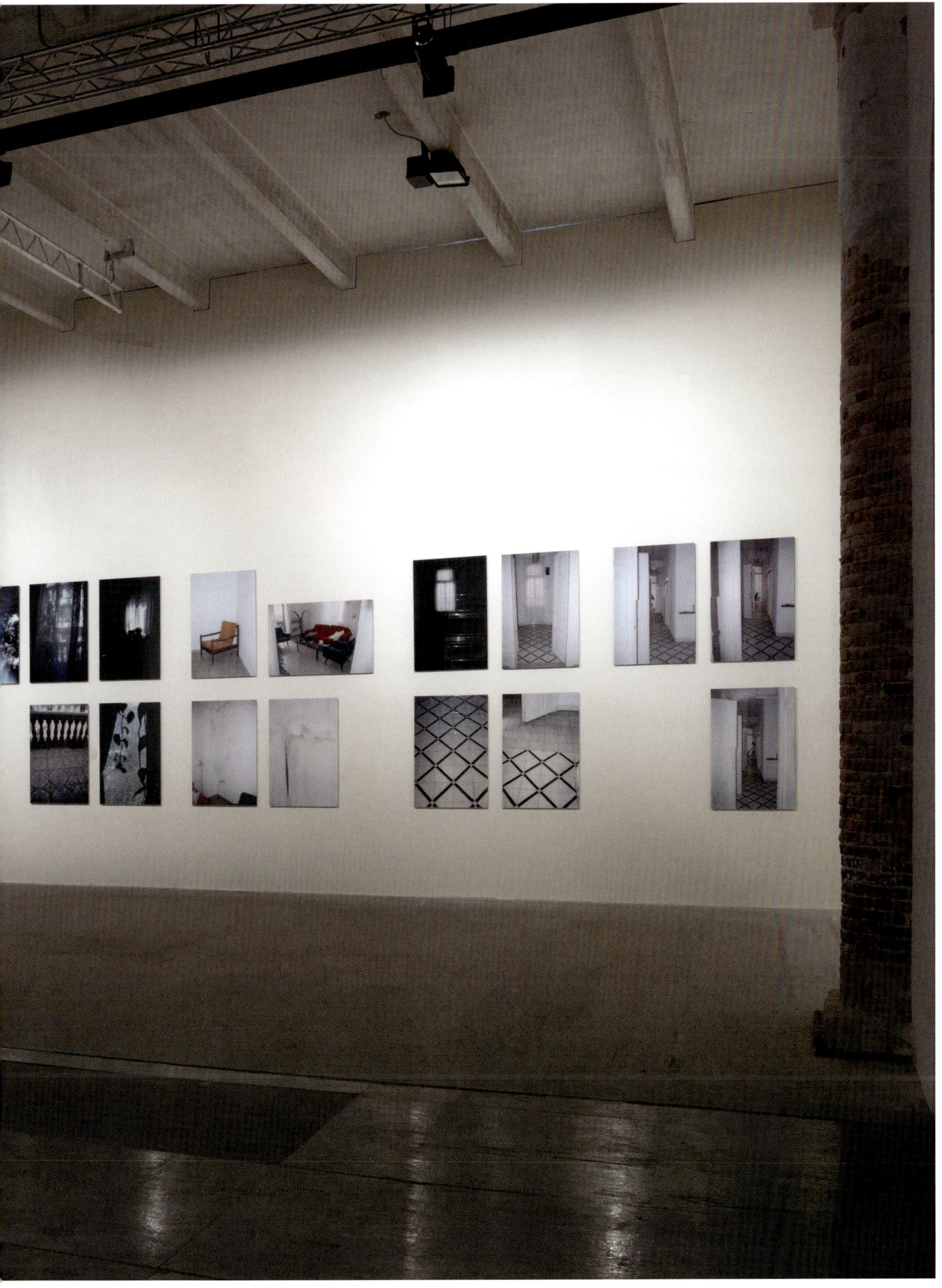

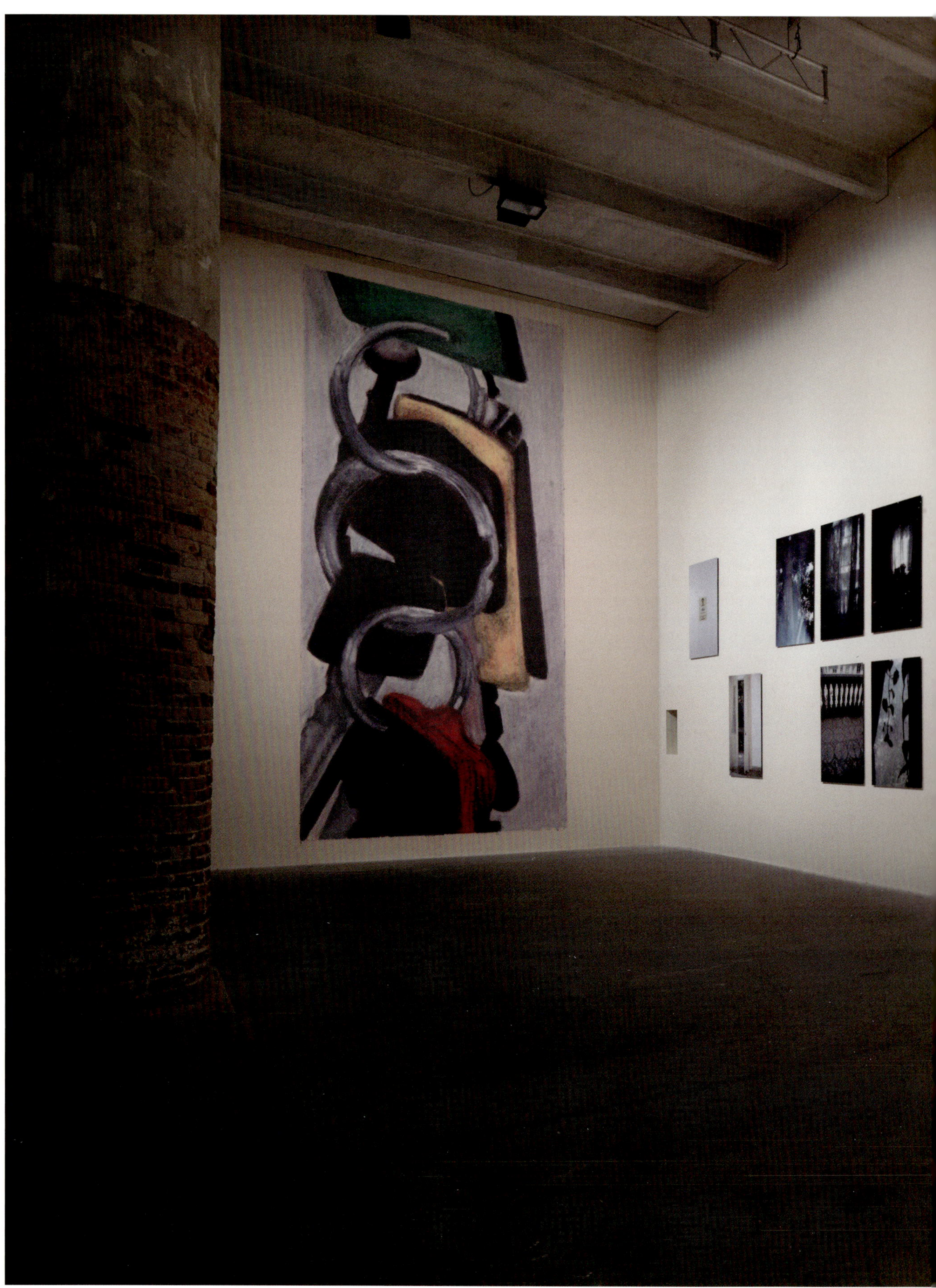

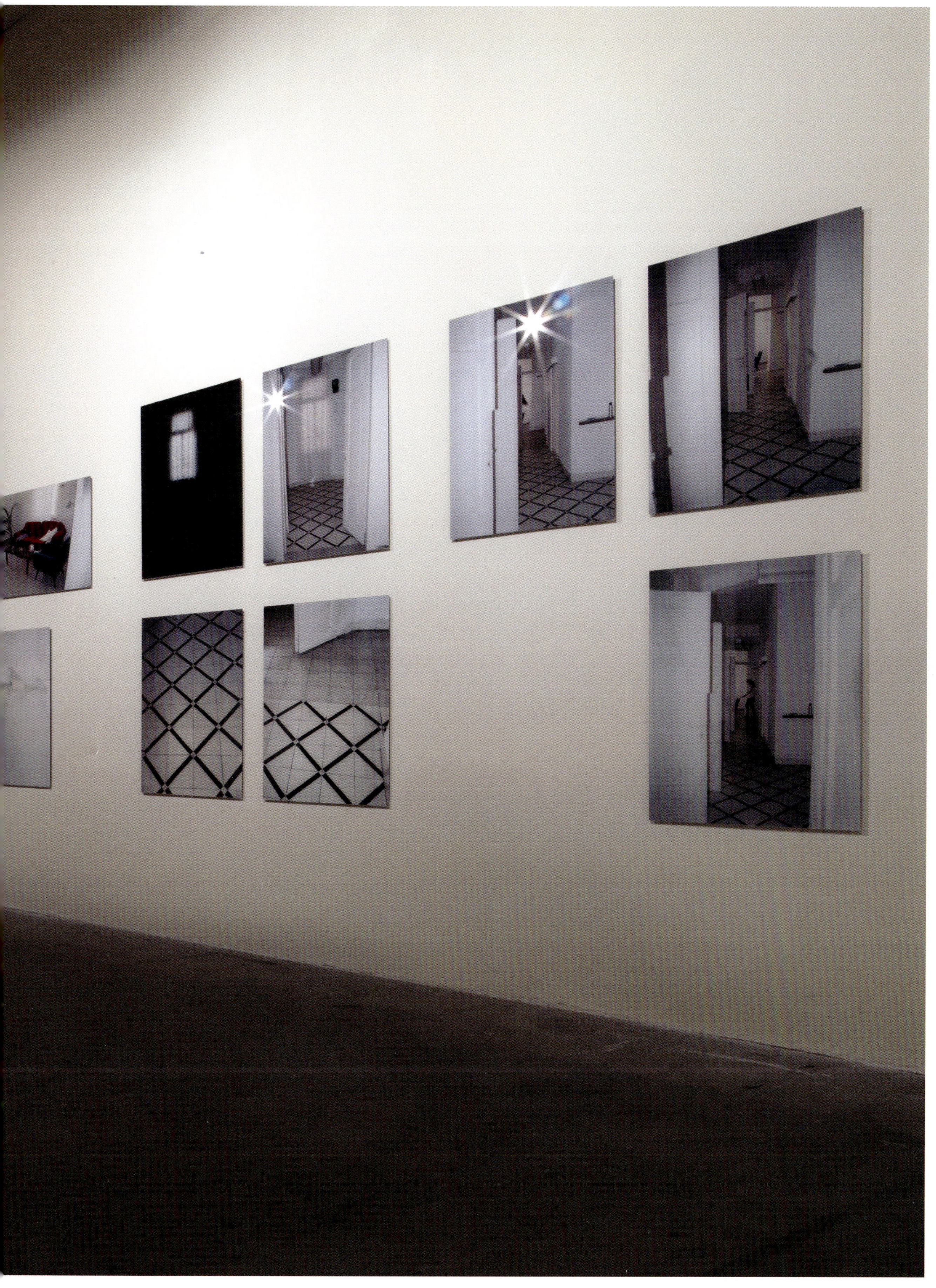

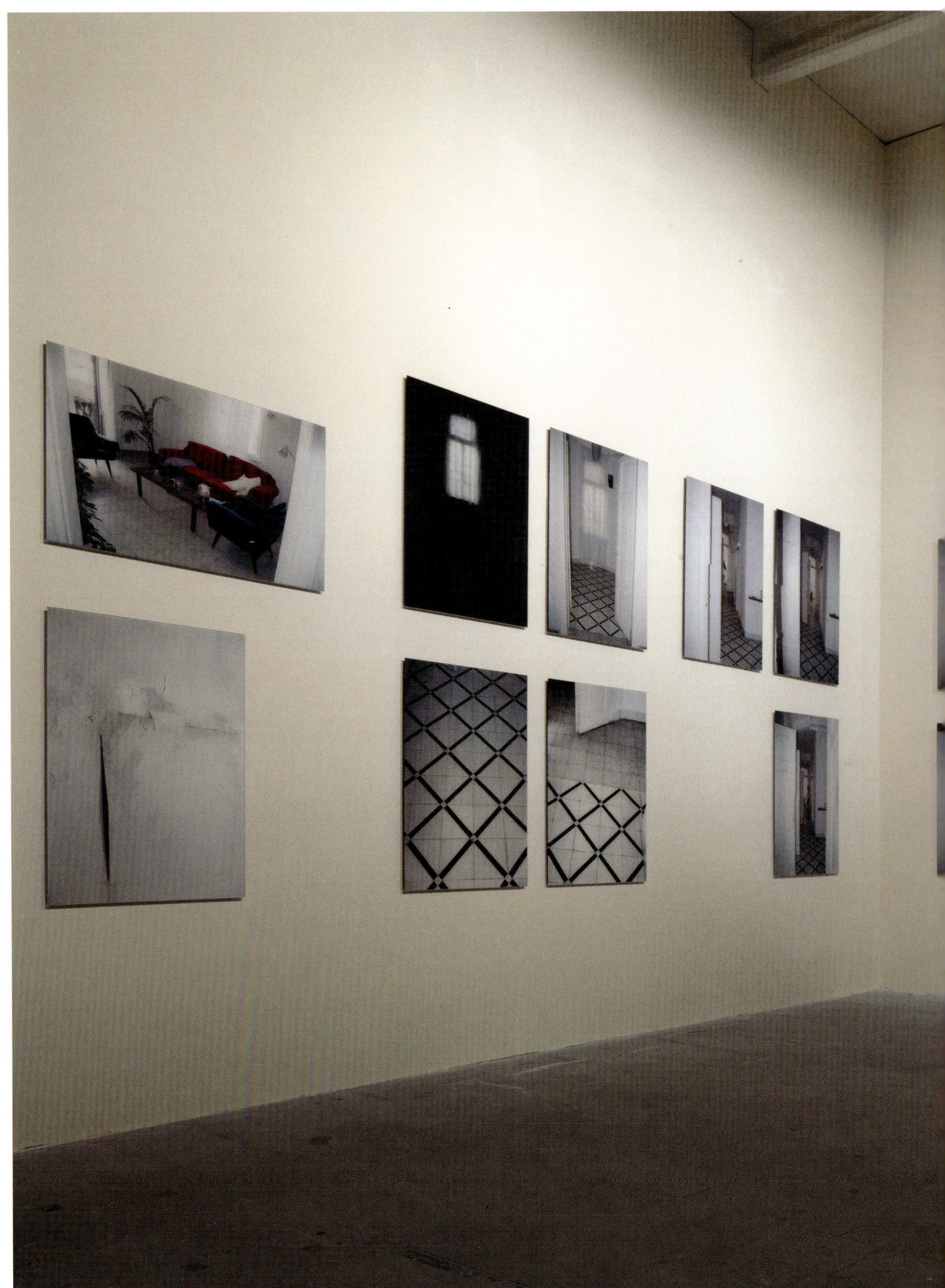

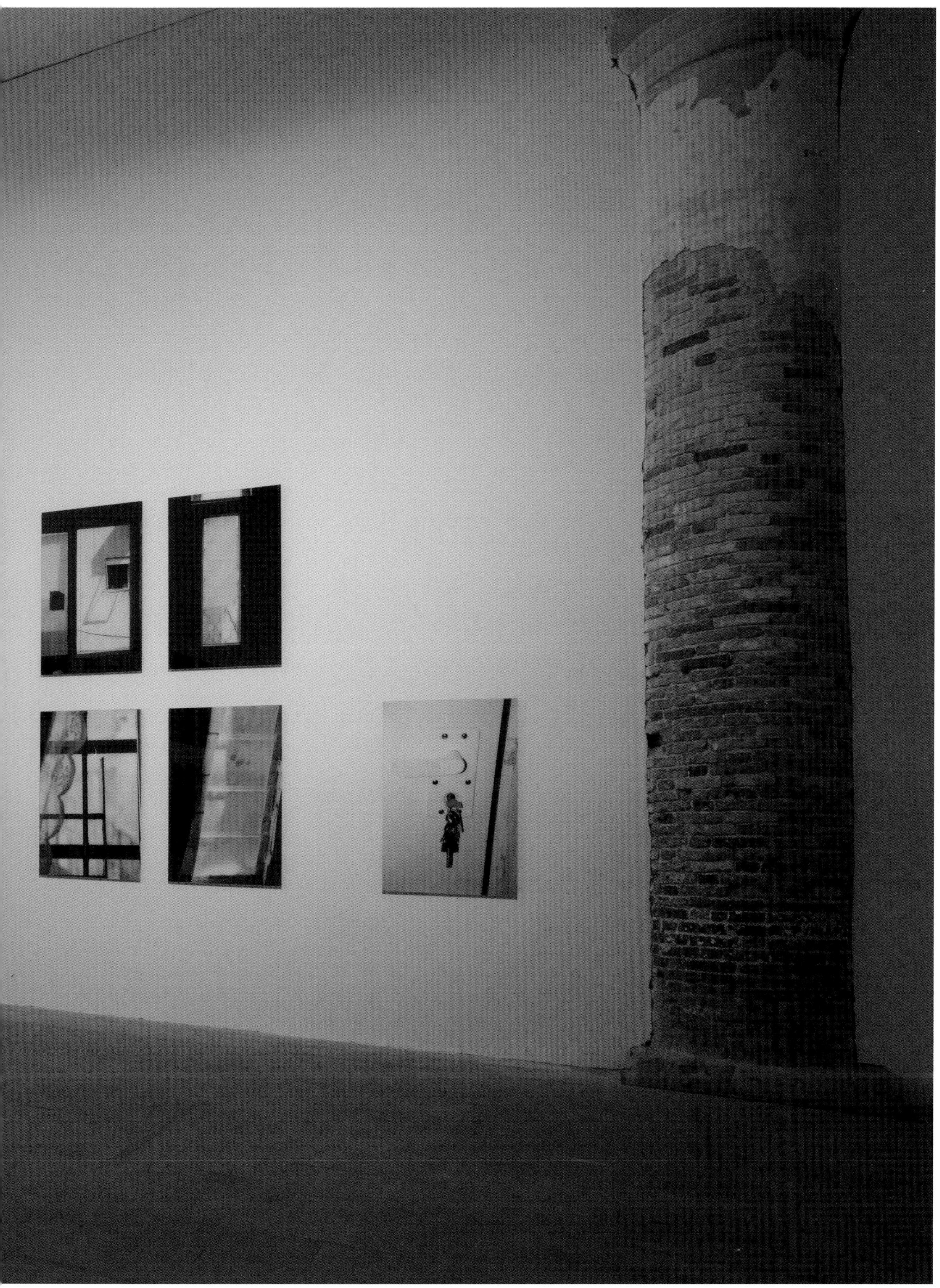

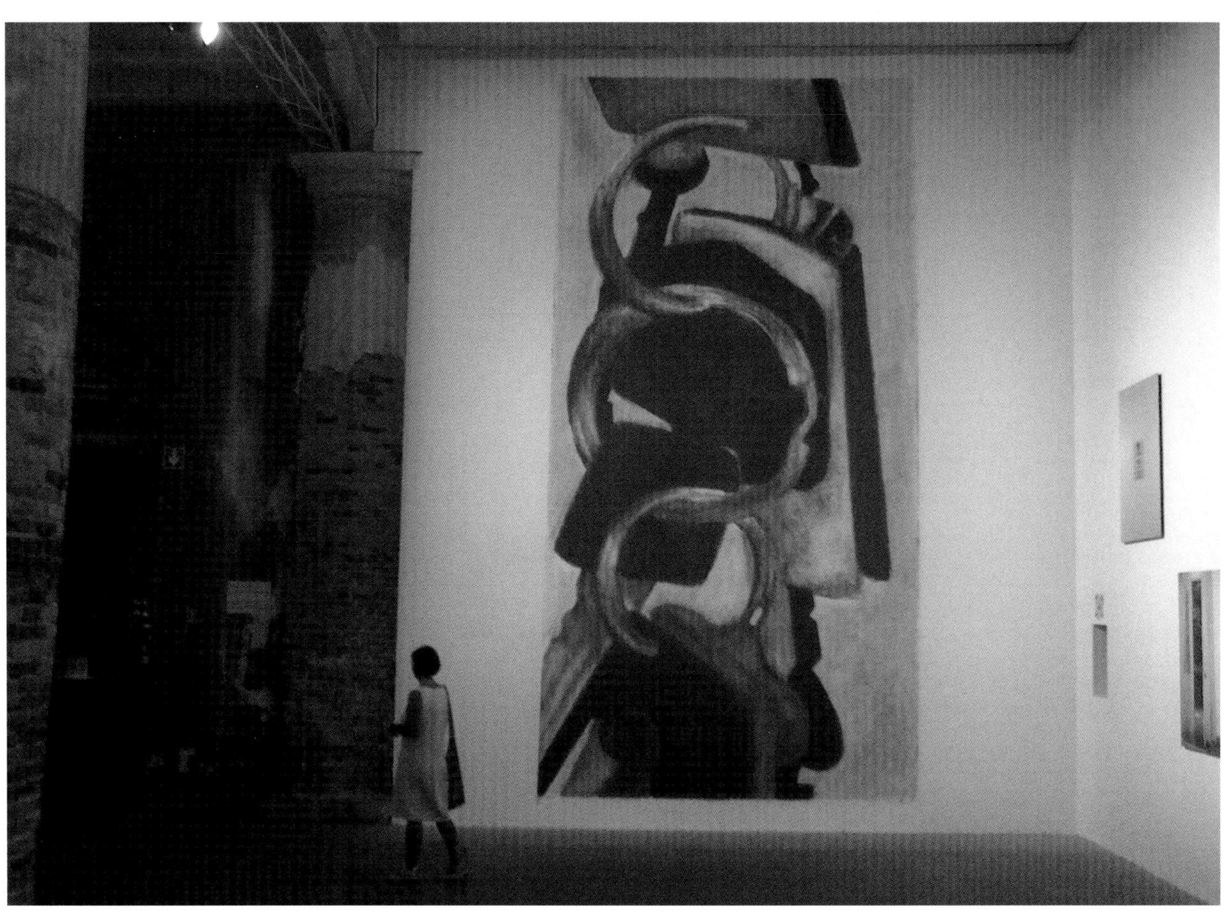

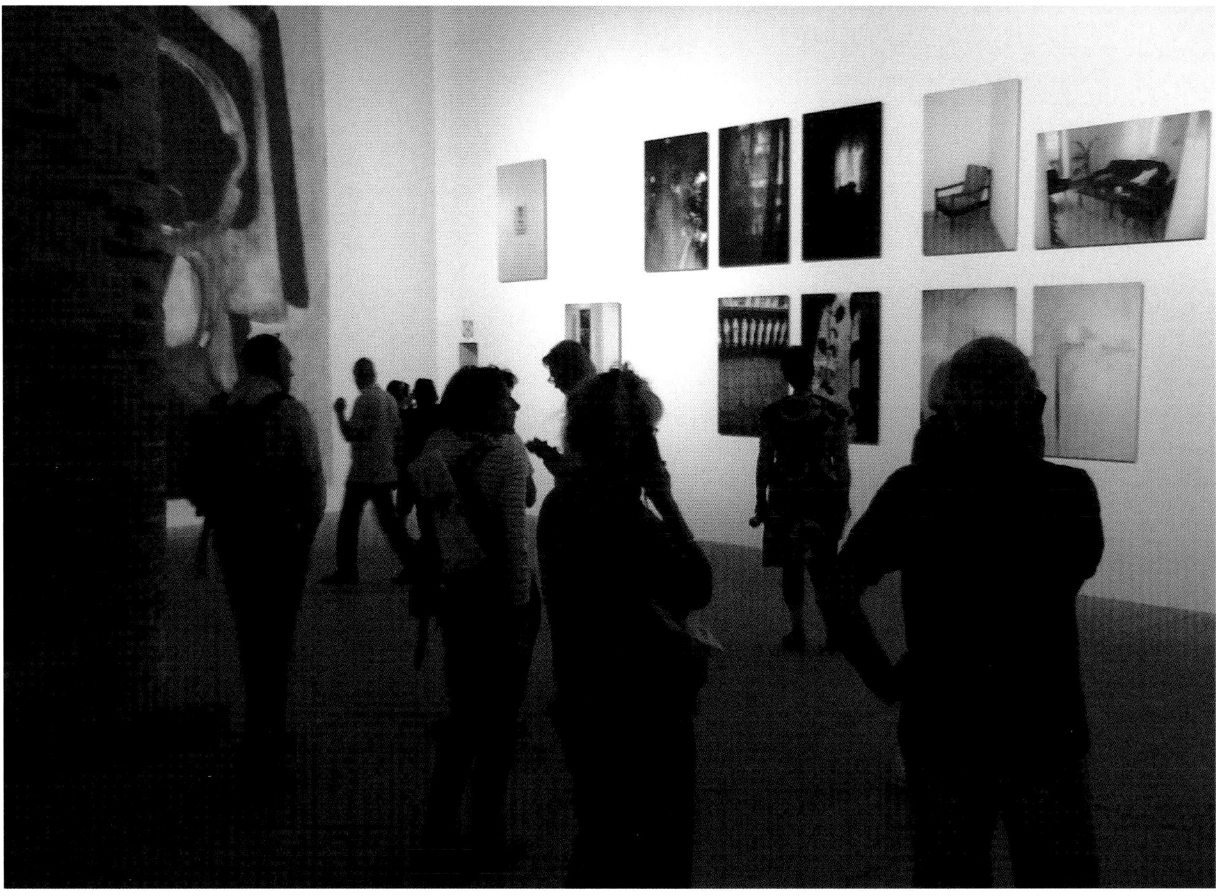

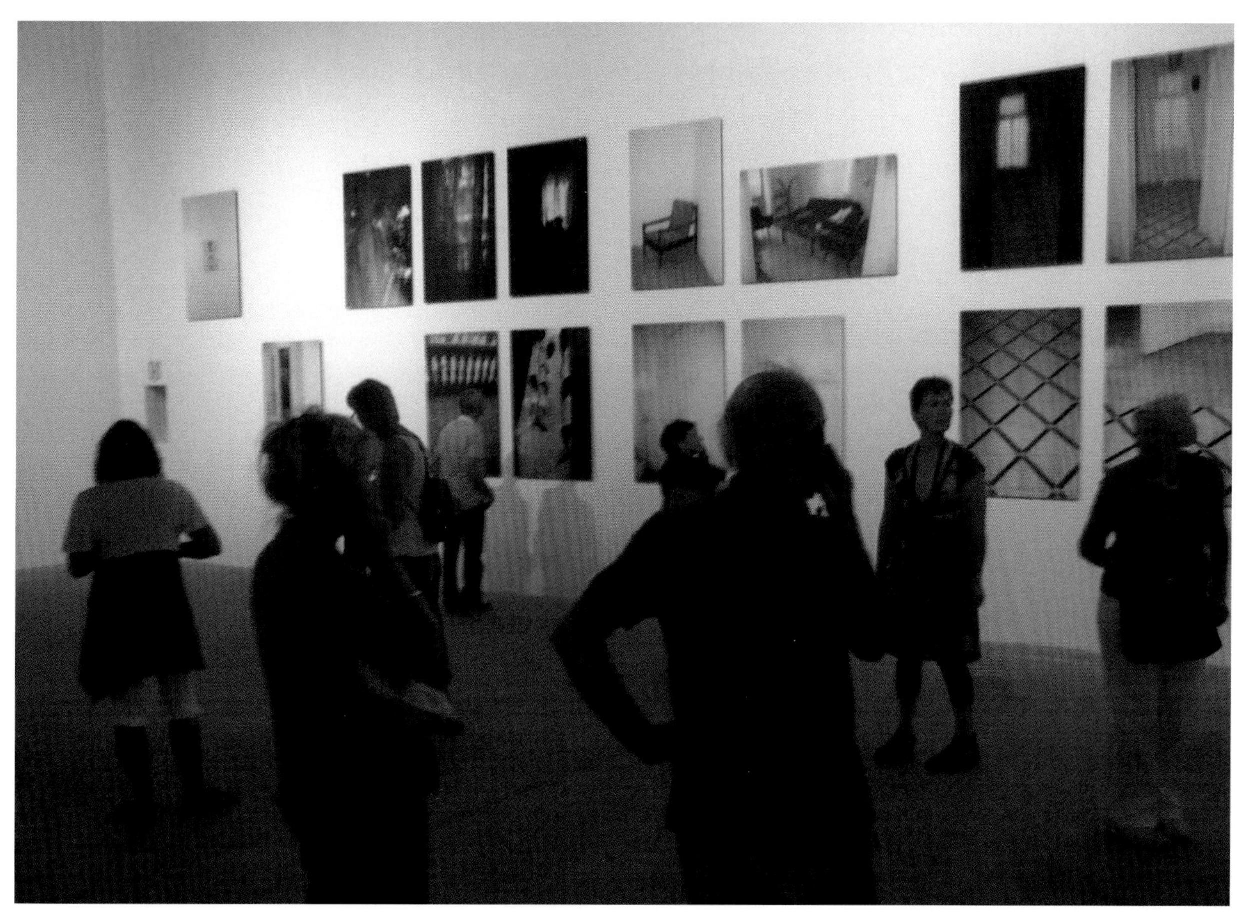

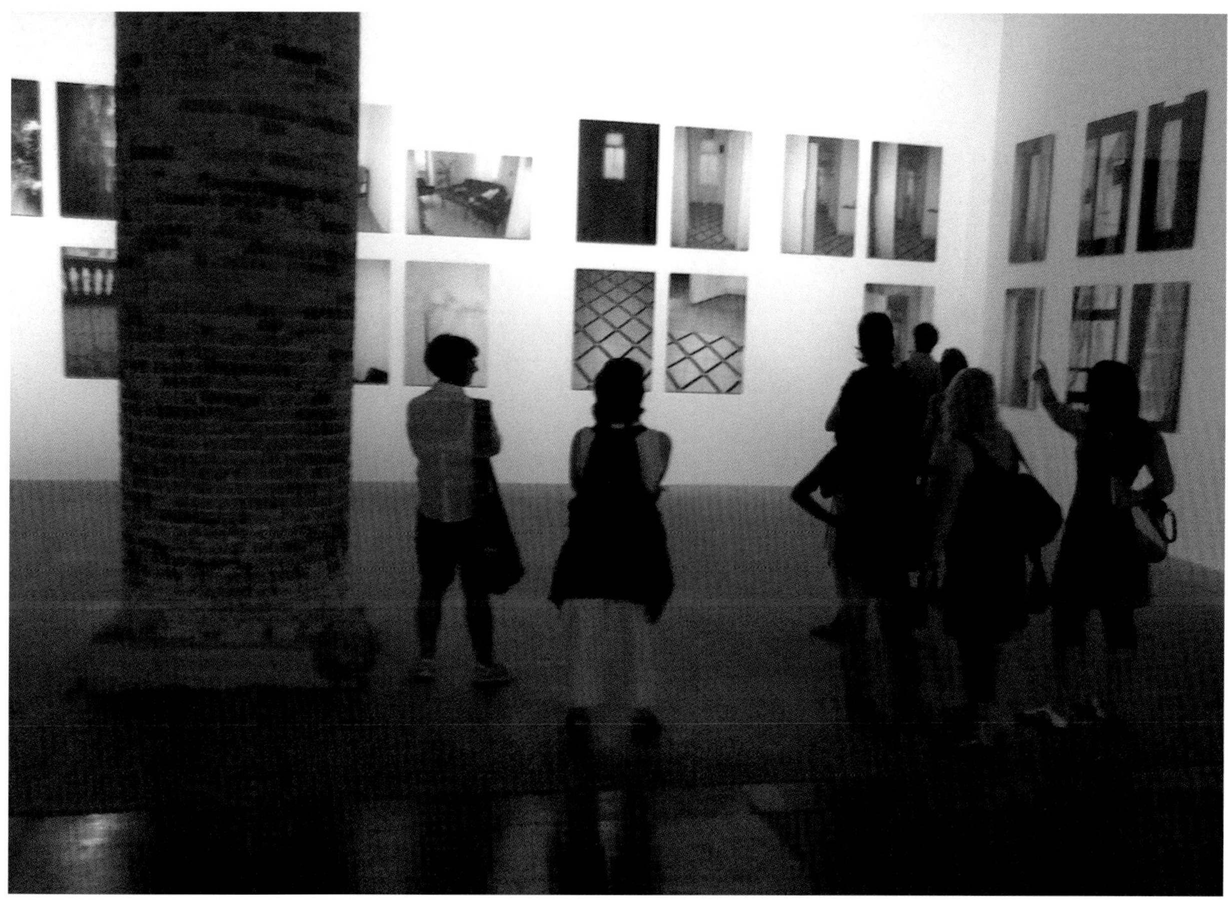

# List of Works

*a different STATE of mind,* No. 1–14 and 16–25, 2009
C-prints, 120 x 80 cm

*a different STATE of mind,* No. 15, 2009
C-print, 80 x 120 cm

Drawings:
*a different STATE of mind,* I–XXIV, 2009
Colored pencil on paper, 10 x 5 cm

*Epilogue,* No. E1, E2, E5, 2009
C-prints, 90 x 60 cm

*Epilogue,* No. E3, E4, 2009
C-prints, 60 x 90 cm

53rd Venice Biennale
Installation photographs: Wolfgang Guenzel, pp. 70–75

Cover illustration:
*a different STATE of mind,* No. 20, 2009
C-print, 120 x 80 cm

Endpapers:
Wallpaper, No. 14 and No. 17, 2009
Site Specific

# Biographies

AMY SIMON

has been deeply involved in fine arts for thirty years. Her career as an exhibiting artist began in 1996 in Stockholm, Sweden. She now divides her time between there and New York City. To date, she has exhibited extensively in Scandinavia, Paris, New York, and also Venice, of which the latter is the subject of this book. Her work is in numerous collections, including Moderna Museet, Stockholm. The evolution of her work, from drawing to photo-collage, to photography, and back to drawing parallels her relationship with the locales that comprise the essence of her artwork. She draws on her personal experiences, memories, and interpretations of the physical world, through PLACE, and all that it inhabits, to understand and explain the intimacies, relevance, and importance of the world around us.

DANIEL BIRNBAUM

is a writer, philosopher, curator, and teacher based in Frankfurt am Main, Germany, where he is the director of the Städelschule Art Academy and its Portikus Gallery. He is the co-founder of the Institut für Kunstkritik, and a member of the board of Frankfurt am Main's Institut für Sozialforschung. His curating has been witnessed at several Trienniales and Biennales in the past years, including in Moscow, and Torino. Most recently, he was the director of the 53rd Venice Biennale *Making Worlds.* Birnbaum is the author of *As a Weasel Sucks Eggs: An Essay on Melancholy and Cannibalism,* and *Chronology,* and has also collaborated on over a dozen titles. He is a contributing editor to *Artforum.*

AMY BAKER SANDBACK

is the director of collection research, Dia Art Foundation. She is a director of *Artforum International Magazine,* and a curator concerned with contemporary culture worldwide.

This book is published in conjunction with the project
*a different STATE of mind,* which premiered in the exhibition
*Making Worlds* at the 53rd Venice Biennale (Arsenale), 2009.
Amy Simon
www.amysimon.net
with thanks to Andrea Meislin Gallery

Copyediting: Alix Sharma-Weigold and Bish Sharma
Graphic design and typesetting: Sandra Praun, Designstudio S, Stockholm
Typeface: Sabon and Univers
Production: Angelika Hartmann, Hatje Cantz
Paper: Galaxi Supermat, 170 g/m$^2$ and Alster Werkdruck, 80 g/m$^2$
Reproductions and printing: Dr. Cantz'sche Druckerei, Ostfildern
Binding: Verlagsbuchbinderei Dieringer, Gerlingen



Published by
Hatje Cantz Verlag
Zeppelinstrasse 32
73760 Ostfildern
Germany
Tel. +49 711 4405-200
Fax +49 711 4405-220
www.hatjecantz.com

Hatje Cantz books are available internationally at selected bookstores.
For more information about our distribution partners please visit
our homepage at www.hatjecantz.com.

ISBN 978-3-7757-2622-1

Printed in Germany

Cover illustration: *a different STATE of mind,* No. 20, 2009

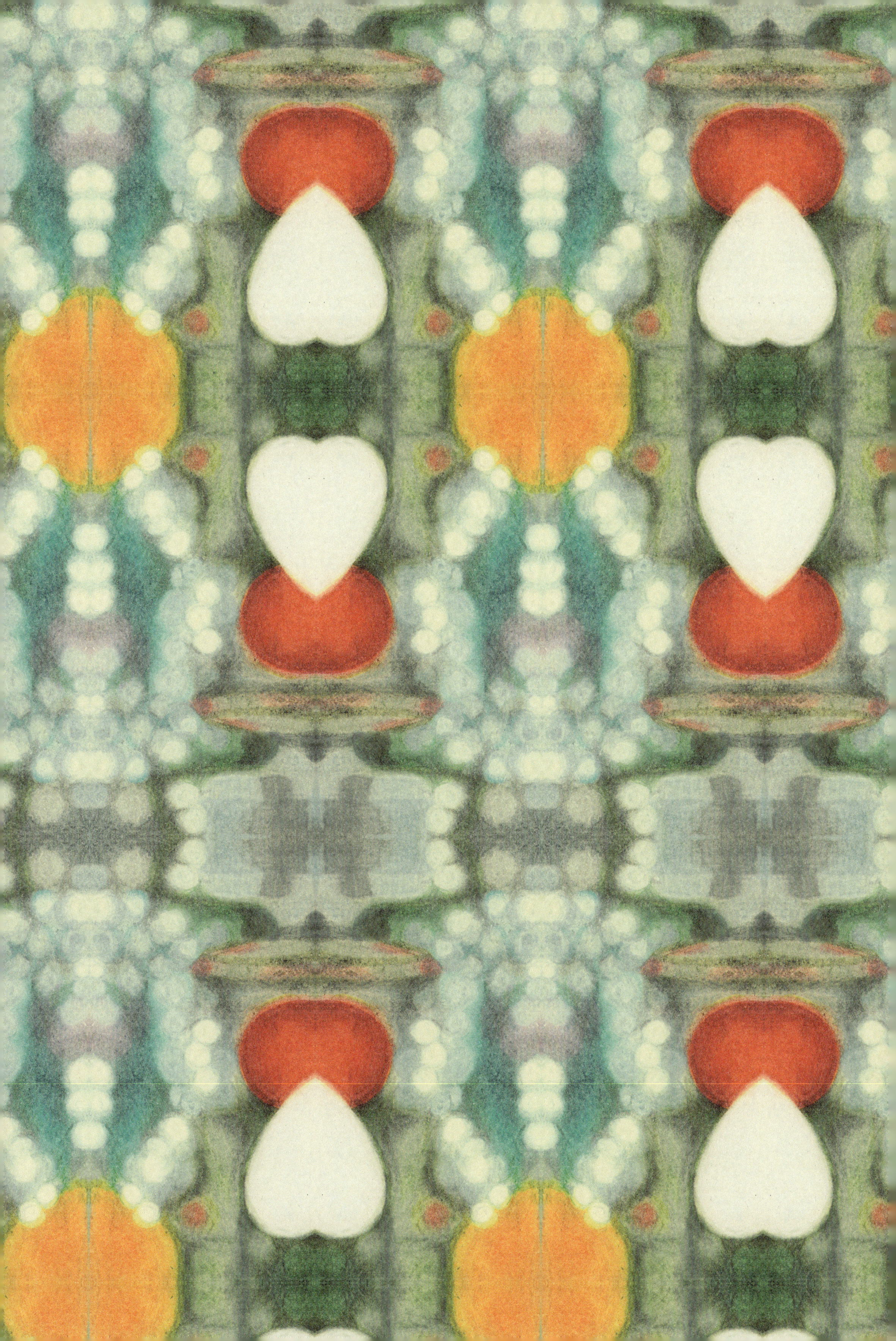

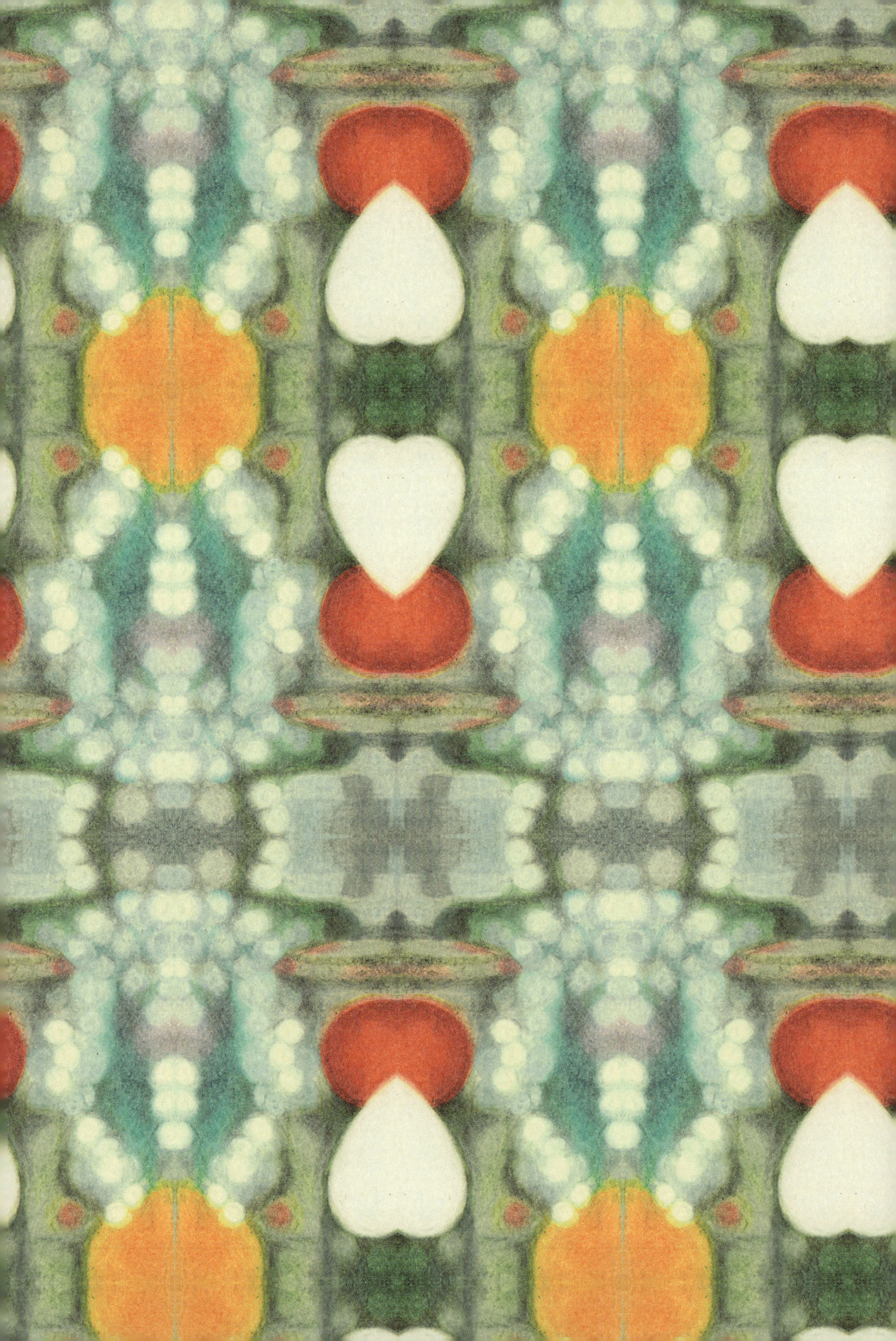